Mississippi Flavors include:

— Magnolias
— Magnificent Antebellum Mansions
— Matchless Delta Blues Music
— Sensational Gulf Coast Vacation Spots
— Splendid Opportunities To Enjoy The Good Life
— Self-Possessed, Independent People
— Superb, Distinctively Southern Food

GREAT FLAVORS OF MISSISSIPPI IS DEDICATED TO THE MARVELOUS PEOPLE OF THE MAGNOLIA STATE WHO HAVE MADE COOKING THE MISSISSIPPI WAY, THE MARVELOUS ART THAT IT IS!

SOUTHERN FLAVORS PUBLICATIONS

P. O. Box 922
Pine Bluff, Arkansas 71613

Copyright 1986

Southern Flavors, Inc.

Please use the order form in the back of the book to order additional copies of GREAT FLAVORS OF MISSISSIPPI, and other cookbooks in the Great Flavors series!

WATCH FOR NEW PUBLICATIONS FROM SOUTHERN FLAVORS, INC.

ISBN 0-9618137-0-9

USA

In Loving Memory of Buddy —
Husband, Father, Son, and Friend

FOREWORD

When we think of Mississippi, we remember many happy times, much loved friends and relatives, the beauty of Mississippi's towns and rivers and Gulf Coast, the Delta and that marvelous scent of freshly harvested cotton, and particularly, that wonderful Mississippi cooking. Our good times in Mississippi have most often either started or ended with good food! GREAT FLAVORS OF MISSISSIPPI is the result of our attachment to Mississippi and Mississippi's marvelous cooks!

GREAT FLAVORS OF MISSISSIPPI is a celebration of the distinctiveness of Mississippi cooks' cooking and features over 200 thoughtfully selected "best recipes" from Mississippi homes, Mississippi's premier industries, and Mississippi restaurants. We have included some intriguing facts about Mississippi and famous Mississippians of note along with the annual dates of many of Mississippi's festivals. We want to thank Mississippi's Research and Development Center, Department of Agriculture and Commerce, Department of Economic Development, and Division of Tourism for the assistance that we received in assimilating the fascinating data and information about the state.

GREAT FLAVORS is a wonderful gift for a Mississippi native, gives a definite flavor of Mississippi to the non-native, and is a marvelous memento to the visitor of the splendid times and superb food that can be had in Mississippi!! We invite you to savor and enjoy!!

Lacey Morris, Co-Editor, Jackson, Mississippi   Jeanne Verlenden, Editor

SOUTHERN FLAVORS, INC.

TABLE OF CONTENTS

APPETIZERS
AND
BEVERAGES

CRAB MEAT DIP

1 (8 oz.) pkg. cream cheese, softened
1 (6 oz.) can crab meat
2 Tbsps. onion, chopped
1 Tbsp. milk
½ tsp. cream-style horseradish
Salt and pepper to taste
¾-1 cup slivered almonds

Mix well first six ingredients. Pour mixture into a small baking dish, and top with the almonds. Heat for 15 minutes at 375°. Serve with Triscuits. Absolutely divine!!

Virginia Primos, Jackson, Mississippi

DELICIOUS CHEESE-N-BEEF BALL

2 (8 oz.) pkgs. Philadelphia cream cheese, softened
1 large bunch green onions, tops and all, chopped
1 small can ripe olives, sliced
1 small can mushrooms, drained and chopped (optional)
3 Tbsps. Accent
1 (2½ oz.) jar dried beef, chopped
Parsley for garnish

Mix together well all ingredients. Shape into a large ball. Garnish with parsley. At Christmas garnish with several springs of holly for a festive look! Serve with Ritz or any party crackers. Men love this!!

Kittye Wright, Columbus, Mississippi

FABULOUS FRUIT SCOOP-UP

8 ozs. *Kraft Marshmallow Cream*
1 (8 oz.) pkg. *Philadelphia Cream*
  Cheese, softened
2½ *Tbsps. orange juice*

1 tsp. *nutmeg or ginger (optional)*
Variety of fresh fruit, cut into
  chunky pieces

Combine first 3 ingredients and half a teaspoon of either nutmeg or ginger. Mix together *well*. Pour the scoop-up mixture into serving bowl. Refrigerate until ready to use. Fruits that are wonderful with the scoop-up include strawberries, apples, honeydew melons, bananas, pineapples, pears, green grapes, and oranges. The fruit looks very pretty, surrounding the scoop-up, alternating fruits according to color. Then, all that's needed are round toothpicks for scooping!! This is a perfectly marvelous appetizer which is also unique! Easy to prepare.

Agnes Bowe, Mineral Wells, Mississippi

MISSISSIPPI FACT:

Mississippi is blessed with five distinct land areas which are "The Hills" (Northeast Mississippi), "The Delta" (Northwest Mississippi), "The Plains" (East Central Mississippi), "The Heartland" (Central and Southwest Mississippi), and "The Gulf Coast" (South and Coastal Mississippi).

GRANDMOTHER LARUE'S SHRIMP DIP

3 (3 oz.) pkgs. cream cheese
2 (5 oz.) cans shrimp
1 cup mayonnaise
Juice of ½ lemon

2 tsps. onion, grated
1 tsp. sugar
1 Tbsp. Worcestershire sauce
Red pepper to taste

Mix all ingredients together well. Wonderful with all kinds of crackers and chips!! Keep refrigerated.

Susan Pratt, Jackson, Mississippi

HELEN'S FAMOUS DIP

1 lb. Velveeta cheese
1 lb. sausage, cooked and drained
4 Tbsps. butter
½ onion, chopped
½ green pepper, chopped

1 (10 oz.) can Rotel tomatoes,
  chopped and drained
Worcestershire sauce
Soy sauce
Oregano

Melt cheese in the top of a double boiler, saute onion and green pepper in butter, and add to cheese, stirring well. Then, add tomatoes, sauces, and oregano to taste. Add sausage, and gently stir until well blended. Serve hot with your favorite chips. WONDERFUL!!

Helen Dalehite, Jackson, Mississippi

8

MERRY CHRISTMAS HORS D'OEUVRES

3 (8 oz.) pkgs. cream cheese
2 sticks butter
1 cup sour cream
1 cup sugar
2 envelopes plain gelatin

½ cup cold water
1 cup white raisins
1 cup slivered almonds, toasted
Rinds of 3 lemons, grated

Blend cream cheese, butter, sour cream, and sugar. Soften envelopes of gelatin in the water. Dissolve gelatin in the top of a double boiler, and add to cream cheese mixture. Add remaining ingredients. Pour mixture into a 2-quart mold; chill in the refrigerator. When firm, remove from mold, and serve with saltine or your favorite crackers. Garnish with rotunda holly. So pretty, festive, and tasty!!

Mary Sharp Rayner, Oxford, Mississippi

MISSISSIPPI FESTIVAL:

Luminaries on the Bayou, held in Inverness, Mississippi, in December, is a marvelous Christmas Eve display of more than 2,000 candles which illuminate both sides of Lake Bradley for more than a mile through the town.

MEXICAN LAYERED DIP

3 avocados, pitted and mashed (in blender or by hand)
2 Tbsps. lemon juice (Fresh is best.)
Salt and pepper
1 cup sour cream
½ cup mayonnaise
2 cans bean dip
1 bunch green onions, tops and all, chopped
3 tomatoes, chopped
1 (6 oz.) can black pitted olives, chopped
1 (8 oz.) pkg. sharp Cheddar cheese, grated
1 can Picante sauce

To mashed avocados, add lemon juice, salt, and pepper. In a separate bowl, combine sour cream and mayonnaise. Spread bean dip in a 9x13-inch baking dish. Top dip first with avocado mixture, and then, sour cream mixture. Sprinkle onions, tomatoes, and olives over sour cream. Then, cover with grated cheese; top with Picante sauce. Serve with chips.

"Men love this, and it's great for weekend and football watching get togethers!!"

Kelly Pratt, Jackson, Mississippi

MISSISSIPPI FACT:

The city of Jackson, Mississippi's capital, was one of the first planned cities in the United States. The building of Jackson began in 1822.

LYNN'S CHEESE BALL

1 (8 oz.) pkg. cream cheese, softened
2 Tbsps. bottled steak sauce
1 cup pecans, finely chopped
1 clove garlic, minced
Several drops of Tabasco
Paprika and parsley flakes for garnish

Beat first 5 ingredients together until well blended. Form mixture into a ball; then, cover with waxed paper, and chill until firm. When firm, remove waxed paper, and garnish with paprika and parsley flakes. Serve with crackers. Outstanding!

Linda Scarborough, Columbus, Mississippi

WONDERFUL HAM-N-CHEESE BALL

1 can Hormel chunk ham
2 (8 oz.) pkgs. cream cheese
1 small bunch green onions, chopped
Louisiana hot sauce to taste
Dry mustard to taste
Garlic powder to taste
Chopped pecans

Mix well first 6 ingredients together. Shape mixture into a ball, and roll in pecans. For a delightfully different taste, substitute sliced, stuffed green olives for the pecans. Serve with your favorite crackers. GREAT!!

Dr. Calvin R. Simmons, Native of Cleveland, Mississippi

MISSISSIPPI VEGETABLE DUNK

1 envelope Lipton Tomato-Onion Soup Mix	1 tsp. soy sauce
1 pt. (16 oz.) sour cream	1 Tbsp. lemon juice
½ tsp. hot pepper sauce	Garlic salt to taste
1 tsp. Worcestershire sauce	

Combine, and mix well all the ingredients. Then, serve with your favorite raw vegetables, and "dunk" to your heart's content! Outstanding!

"The Mississippi Vegetable Dunk is delicious in its "pure form." It is also a great "starter dip" as you can add shrimp, crab meat, cream cheese, or really just about anything that you know would be good with the dunk in its pure form!"

Lacey Morris, GREAT FLAVORS OF MISSISSIPPI

MISSISSIPPI FACT:

During the last century more than half of the millionaires in the United States lived in the town houses and plantation homes of Natchez!

SIDNEY'S DIP

2 lbs. processed cheese
1 large onion
1 (8 oz.) can jalapeno peppers

1 bud garlic (I use minced garlic.)
1 qt. mayonnaise

Grind first 4 ingredients in a food processor (or chop and blend in blender), and mix into mayonnaise. For absolute best taste, chill at least 24 hours before serving. Serve with favorite chips or crackers. *Yields about 2 quarts.*

Mayor Sidney Runnels, Canton, Mississippi

WONDERFUL CHEESE SPREAD

1½ lbs. *New York sharp cheese,*
  grated
2 oz. *Frank's Louisiana Hot Sauce*
1 *medium onion, grated*

1 (4 oz.) jar pimentos and juice
1 tsp. garlic powder
1 pint Hellmann's mayonnaise

Puree onion, pimentos, and juice in a blender. Add cheese, hot sauce, garlic powder, and mayonnaise to onion-pimento mixture, and beat until fluffy. Put in a sealed container, and refrigerate. Mixture will "set up" while chilling. Serve with melba rounds. This dip makes a great, spicy pimento cheese sandwich!!

Susie W. Cook, Columbus, Mississippi

MOMMA HATTIE'S CHEESE KRISPIES

2 sticks margarine, softened
2 cups sharp Cheddar cheese,
  grated

2 cups flour
1/8 tsp. cayenne pepper
2 cups Rice Krispies

Mix together well the margarine and cheese; set aside. Blend flour and pepper, and add to the cheese mixture. Stir in Rice Krispies; then, form into very small balls, place on an ungreased cookie sheet, and press each ball once with a fork. Bake at 350° for 12 to 15 minutes. Krispies should be very light brown. Cool before removing from cookie sheet. These cheese krispies are wonderful topped with a hot garlic pickle slice (recipe on page 16)!!

Hattie Barnhill, Starkville, Mississippi

REAL MISSISSIPPI FOLK'S FACT:

Mississippi folk know that two names are better than one—Bobby Joe, Mary Alice, Kathy Lou, Billy Wayne!

EGGPLANT CAVIAR

1 medium eggplant	2 tsps. salt
1 large onion, chopped	1 tsp. pepper
1 green pepper, chopped	¼ tsp. cayenne pepper
2 large garlic cloves, crushed	¼ tsp. Worcestershire sauce
½ cup olive oil	1 tsp. Accent
2 tomatoes	2 Tbsps. dry white wine

Punch several holes in eggplant, and place in a shallow pan with a small amount of water. Bake at 400⁰ until soft (about an hour). Saute onion, green pepper, and garlic in hot oil until tender (but not brown). Peel and chop eggplant and tomatoes; add to sauteed mixture. Then, add salt, peppers, Worcestershire, and Accent. Add wine. Mix everything thoroughly, and continue to cook gently until mixture is fairly thick. Cool; then place in the refrigerator. Serve chilled with rye crackers and rye party bread. DELICIOUS!

"This delightful appetizer is also very good served as a side dish with a meat entree. Just top with pats of butter and Parmesan cheese, and heat in a casserole dish until hot and bubbly."

Nancy Stovall, Stovall, Mississippi

GARLIC PICKLES

1 gallon SOUR (not dill)
  pickles
5 lbs. sugar

2/3 cup apple cider vinegar
1 box garlic, separated into pods
2 pkgs. mixed pickling spice

Drain pickles, slice into rounds, and layer with sugar in the jar they came in; let stand for 24 hours. Drain sugar off into a large pot; add vinegar. Let boil for 10 to 15 minutes. Put sliced pickles, garlic, and spices alternately in a big jar, and pour hot sugar/vinegar mixture over them; let stand for 24 hours. Drain syrup off into a large pot, and transfer pickles to smaller pint jars. Heat syrup again, and pour over pickles in the pint jars. Seal.

From the Recipe Collection of Mrs. G. Garland Lyell
Jackson, Mississippi

HOT GARLIC PICKLES

1 (32 oz.) jar of name brand sliced
  dill pickles
2 cups sugar

4-8 toes garlic, sliced in half
½ small bottle Tabasco (1 small
  bottle to make lethal)

Drain all pickle juice from jar; add remaining ingredients to jar; reseal. Place jar upright on a kitchen counter the first day, place upside down the second, and continue this for 5 days. These pickles are great on a cheese cracker or straight out of the jar!!

Chester Harvey, Ocean Springs, Mississippi

SALTY, BOILED PEANUTS

1-2 Tbsp. salt per lb. of peanuts to   Water to cover
be salted (Use 2 Tbsps. if you
desire really salty peanuts!)

Salt the water; add the peanuts, and cook slowly for 2 to 3 hours. Then, turn burner off, and let the peanuts cool in the salty water to absorb the salt. Then, enjoy!!

Nell Cody, Farmer's Market, Jackson, Mississippi

TOASTED PECANS

Pecans, shelled and halved   Salt
Butter, melted

For each cup of pecans, put a tablespoon of butter in a shallow pan. Then, put pecans in, and stir well. Sprinkle with salt; then, brown at 350° for approximately 20 minutes, stirring frequently. Remove from oven, and sprinkle with more salt, if necessary. Spread pecans on paper towels to cool.ABSOLUTELY WONDERFUL!!

Sternberg Pecan Company, Jackson, Mississippi

Sternberg Pecan Company is a wonderful place to order gifts for friends and relatives, particularly at Christmas time!

MISSISSIPPI CAVIAR

*1 gallon black-eyed peas, seasoned
    with salt, pepper, and ham hocks*
1 cup oil
½ cup vinegar
3 bunches green onions, chopped

3 cloves garlic, slivered
Salt and pepper to taste
*1 jar Trappey's Salted Peppers,
    with juice and chopped in
    blender*

Cook peas and seasoning in oil until peas are tender. Then, remove fat, and drain well. Add remaining ingredients to the peas, and gently combine. Put peas mixture in a bowl that can be turned to shake and mix. Then, refrigerate for at least 24 hours. The "caviar" can be kept for 2 weeks and gets better all along!!

"Mississippi Caviar is a must for New Year's Day!"

Nancy Landrum, Columbus, Mississippi

MISSISSIPPI FACTS:
In 1839, Mississippi became the first state to grant women the right to own property separately from their husbands! In Columbus in 1884, Mississippi was the first state to establish a state supported college for women which was originally named Mississippi Industrial Institute and College and is now called Mississippi University for Women.

18

FROZEN PEACH DAIQUIRI

1 cup rum
1 (12 oz.) box frozen peaches

1 pt. crushed ice
1 oz. cointreau

Break up peaches, but do not thaw. Blend all the ingredients for a minute in blender. Serve in frosted wine or champagne glasses. Wonderful!!
Serves 6-8 generously.

Doris Crull, Winona, Mississippi

HETTI'S ROSÉ ICE

1 (6 oz.) can frozen pink lemonade
1 (6 oz.) can Rose' (Use the empty lemonade can.)

Ice cubes

Put lemonade and Rose' in a blender, and fill to the top with ice cubes. Turn the blender on high for several minutes. Absolutely divine!!
Serves 4-6 generously in wine glasses.

"This Rose' Ice is perfect for a ladies' luncheon!"

Lacey Morris, GREAT FLAVORS OF MISSISSIPPI

MISSISSIPPI MINT JULIP

2 tsps. sugar   *Crushed ice*
1½ ozs. bourbon
Fresh mint, 3-4 sprigs of tender
   mint shoots

Dissolve sugar in enough water to form an oily syrup. In a tall glass, crush sprigs until most of the mint's essence has been extracted. Remove mint from glass; then, fill glass with crushed ice, and pour in the bourbon. Allow bourbon to become thoroughly chilled; then, add remaining sugar syrup. Let mixture stand in the glass for a few minutes, but don't stir. Place additional sprigs of fresh mint around the rim of the glass, and serve immediately.

From OLD SOUTHERN SECRETS Cookbook

MISSISSIPPI FACT:

OLD SOUTHERN SECRETS, published in 1915, is one of the earliest Mississippi cookbooks written and published by Mississippians!!

MRS. LYELL'S EGGNOG

8 large fresh eggs
1 Tbsp. sugar to each egg
1 Tbsp. whiskey to each egg

1 pt. whipping cream
Nutmeg, freshly grated

Whip cream, and set aside. In a large bowl, beat egg yolks and half of the sugar together. Beat egg whites stiff, and add the other half of the sugar. Add whiskey to egg yolks; then, fold in egg whites. Lastly, fold in whipped cream, and sprinkle the top with the grated nutmeg. QUITE SIMPLY DELICIOUS!!
Serves 8.

From the Recipes of Mrs. G. Garland Lyell
Jackson, Mississippi

MISSISSIPPI FESTIVAL:

The Mistletoe Market Place, sponsored by the Junior League of Jackson and held at Jackson's Trade Mart, is a Christmas Bazaar that features novelties from many retail stores and a tearoom with wonderful food!

MISSISSIPPI'S BEST BLOODY MARY

1 (46 oz.) can V-8 Juice
18 ozs. vodka
¼ cup Worcestershire sauce

Juice of 3 limes (Use only fresh!!)
24 drops Tabasco
Dash of cumin

Blend all the ingredients together well. Pour over ice. This is *the* absolute best!
Yields 12 8-ounce servings.

Ernest McLaurin, Jackson, Mississippi

WONDERFUL MINT TEA

6 bags Bigelow Plantation Mint
  Tea
Scant cup of sugar

½ cup lemon juice (Fresh is best!)

Bring tea bags to a boil in a cup and a half of boiling water. Steep for 15 minutes. In another cup and a half of boiling water, mix sugar and lemon juice. Combine 2 mixtures, and add enough ice water to make 2 quarts. Delicious and great for luncheons and afternoon teas.

Heritage Antique Club, Jackson, Mississippi

SOUPS, SALADS, AND SANDWICHES

GULF COAST GUMBO

2 Tbsps. bacon grease
2 heaping Tbsps. flour
1 lb. fresh okra, chopped (May use frozen.)
2 large onions, chopped
1 small (#2) can tomatoes
1 qt. chicken stock
2 bay leaves
3 qts. hot water
2 tsps. gumbo file
2 lbs. fresh shrimp, boiled and peeled
1 (6½-7 oz.) can special crab meat or 2 pts. oysters
Ham (optional)

Brown flour in grease until flour's color is very dark. Add okra and onions, cooking until okra is stringy. Add tomatoes, stock, bay leaves, and hot water; cook until vegetables are done. The vegetable mixture for gumbo can be made ahead of time and frozen. Heat vegetable mixture to a boil; add shrimp and crab meat (or oysters). While hot, add gumbo file. Don't overcook!! The gumbo can be kept hot, but don't boil again! Remove bay leaves before serving. WONDERFUL.
Serves 15.

A MISSISSIPPI ROUX

In a saucepan, mix 2/3 cup oil and 2/3 cup flour. Cook, uncovered, until roux is light brown, stirring constantly. Stir, and continue to cook until roux is a dark brown color. Drain off excess grease; stir again. A roux comes in so handy for starting gumbos and soups!

From the Recipes of Eddieth Davis, Pascagoula, Mississippi

CRAB SOUP

1 stick butter	3 soup cans of milk or half and half
½ cup green onions, finely chopped	1 lb. crab meat
1 can cream of mushroom soup	1 lb. crab claw meat
1 can cream of celery soup	2 Tbsps. sherry
1 can cream of chicken soup	Salt and pepper to taste

Combine, and heat all the ingredients together, stirring constantly. The soup is good if made the day before!
Serves 8-10.

Anna Knight, Taylorsville, Mississippi

MISSISSIPPI FACT:

The Gulf Coast is the fastest growing area in Mississippi. Its famous sand beaches have become a vacation paradise which some have called "America's Riviera." As a matter of fact, Mississippi's Gulf Coast is the home of the world's largest manmade beach which is 26 miles long and approximately 200 feet wide!

25

CREAMY MUSHROOM SOUP

6 Tbsps. butter
1 medium onion, finely chopped
1 lb. fresh mushrooms, chopped
3½ Tbsps. flour
½ tsp. meat concentrate or beef
  bouillon cube
2 (14½ oz.) cans Swanson's
  Chicken Broth

1 bay leaf
2 sprigs parsley
Pinch of thyme
⅛ tsp. pepper
¼ cup vermouth
¾ cup light cream

Melt butter, and saute onions; add mushrooms, and cook for 3 to 4 minutes.
Remove mixture from heat; stir in flour. Add next 7 ingredients, bring to a
boil, and simmer for 5 minutes. Stir in cream, and reheat.
Serves 6.

Carolyn McIntyre, Jackson, Mississippi

FRESH ZUCCHINI SOUP

2 lbs. zucchini, finely chopped
½ cup green onions, chopped
2 cloves garlic
4 Tbsps. butter

3 cans chicken broth
1 cup milk
1½ tsps. curry powder or to taste

In a covered saucepan, saute first 3 ingredients in the butter for 10 minutes.
Add remaining ingredients, and stir. Delicious, served hot or cold!
Serves 6.

Donna Knight, Taylorsville, Mississippi

CUCUMBER SOUP

4 cucumbers
2 cups buttermilk
4 scallions, white part only,
  chopped
½ cup parsley, chopped

2 qts. sour cream
2 tsps. salt
¼ cup lemon juice
¼ cup fresh dill

Cut 18 thin and unpeeled slices from one cucumber; set aside. Peel, seed, and chop remaining cucumbers. Place half of the chopped cucumbers in a blender, add a cup of buttermilk, and blend, adding half of the parsley and scallions. Repeat process with the blender again. Pour pureed cucumbers into a large bowl. With a wire whisk, beat in remaining ingredients. Refrigerate. Serve with a slice or two of the cucumber floating on top. *Serves 16-18 generously.*

Margaret Ratelle, St. James Episcopal Church Cooking School
Jackson, Mississippi

SENGELESE SOUP

1 can cream of chicken soup
1 can beef bouillon
1 Tbsp. applesauce

1 tsp. curry powder or to taste
Dash of cinnamon

Combine all ingredients, stirring well. Heat, and serve piping hot. So easy! *Serves 4.*

Amelia Montjoy, Clinton, Mississippi

CREAM OF CORN SOUP WITH ALMONDS

2 cups cream style canned corn	⅛ tsp. salt
1 cup cream	⅛ tsp. pepper
1 cup milk	½ cup almonds, ground
1 onion slice	1-3 drops almond extract
1 Tbsp. butter	Whipped cream
⅛ tsp. cayenne pepper	

Mash corn through a sieve. In a medium sized saucepan, combine cream and milk, peppers, and salt. Then, add corn and onion slice, and gently simmer over low to medium heat until onion is tender, stirring from time to time. Remove onion, and add butter. Then, add almonds and drops of almond extract. Serve with a spoonful of whipped cream floating on top. A truly Southern soup!!

Serves 6-8.

Margaret Ratelle, St. James Episcopal Church Cooking School
Jackson, Mississippi

MISSISSIPPI FACT:
American Indians, which include the Chickasaw, Choctaw, and Natchez tribes of Mississippi, have made very important contributions to today's world food supply. Actually, about half of all the crops now grown were first raised by the Indians and include not only corn but also potatoes, tapioca, sweet potatoes, peanuts, squash, tomatoes, pumpkins, peppers, and several kinds of beans!!

CHEF'S CHOICE MINESTRONE

1 cup assorted dried beans
3 cups meat stock or water seasoned
  with bouillon
1 lb. Italian sausage (or ground beef
  or pork sausage)
2-3 soup bones, trimmed of fat
1 onion, chopped
3-4 celery ribs, chopped
1-2 garlic cloves, minced
1 medium can tomatoes or 2-3 fresh

2-3 bay leaves
Salt and pepper to taste
¼-½ cup red wine (optional)
Hot sauce to taste (optional)
Basil, oregano, fennel, or Italian
  seasoning to taste
½-1 cup pasta, uncooked (your choice
  spaghetti, vermicelli, macaroni)
Parmesan cheese

Soak beans overnight, or use "quick soak" method; Boil beans for 3-5 minutes; take off burner; let beans sit for an hour. Rinse beans, and place in a large, heavy pot with stock; add onion, celery, garlic, and tomatoes, bring to a boil, and reduce heat to simmer. Brown sausage, breaking up with a fork; drain well on paper towels. Sear soup bones in a hot skillet; add bones and crumbled meat to soup. Add bay leaves and other seasonings except for salt and pepper (You may find you don't need them!). Simmer soup for about 2 hours; then, add wine and correct seasonings. If you don't want beans pureed, soup will be cooked. For "soupier" beans, simmer an additional hour. About 5 minutes before serving, mix in pasta. Adjust seasonings; serve as soon as pasta is cooked. Sprinkle with Parmesan cheese. WONDERFUL!!

"The dry bean soup mix, poured into a French canning jar along with the Minestrone Soup recipe and a bouquet garné make a charming Christmas Happy!"
Helen Murphey Austin, Food Editor, ARKANSAS DEMOCRAT, Little Rock, Arkansas
Helen is a graduate of the University of Southern Mississippi and grew up in Hattiesburg.

29

WESTON'S ONION SOUP

3-4 medium white onions, sliced
3-4 medium brown onions, sliced
2-3 Tbsps. butter or bacon fat
1 pt. boiling water
1 qt. beef stock
2 Tbsps. carrots, diced
2 pinches marjoram

1 pinch thyme
1 cup dry red wine
Salt and pepper to taste
3 Tbsps. flour
3 Tbsps. cold water
Toast (optional)
Parmesan Cheese (optional)

Melt butter or fat, and add carrots. Then, add onions, marjoram, and thyme. Cook in the fat until onions become clear in color. Add hot water; simmer, covered, for 20 minutes or until vegetables are tender. Add stock and wine. Blend flour and cold water, adding some of the hot liquid; mix this well, and stir into the soup; boil for a few minutes. Add salt and pepper (Be discreet with the pepper and careful with the salt!). Pour into soup bowls, place a slice of toast on top, and sprinkle with Parmesan cheese. Place under broiler until cheese melts, and serve. Truly delicious!!
Serves 6-8.

Dr. Heber Simmons, Jr., Jackson, Mississippi

HAWAIIAN CHICKEN SALAD

1 cup mandarin oranges
1 cup chunk pineapple
1 cup seedless green grapes
  (Can use canned grapes.)
1 cup mayonnaise

1 fryer, cooked, boned and chopped
1 cup celery, chopped
1 cup chow mein noodles
1 cup lettuce, shredded

Mix together the first 6 ingredients. Then, just before serving, stir in the noodles and lettuce. HEAVENLY!!

Trudy Wiggins, Pascagoula, Mississippi

CHICKEN RICE SALAD

2 Tbsps. lemon juice
¾ cup mayonnaise
2 cups long-grain rice, cooked
2 cups chicken, cooked and diced
1 cup celery, diced
½ cup pimento-stuffed olives, sliced

¼ cup almonds, sliced and toasted
2 Tbsps. green onions and tops,
  thinly sliced
Dash of salt and pepper
6 lettuce cups and peeled tomato
  halves (optional)

Combine lemon juice and mayonnaise; blend well. Combine mayonnaise mixture with remaining ingredients, excluding lettuce cups or tomatoes. Serve on lettuce cups or tomato halves, and garnish with whole olives. *Serves 6 generously.*

TREASURES

2 cups mayonnaise
½ cup horseradish, drained
½ tsp. MSG
2 tsps. dry mustard
2 tsps. lemon juice
½ tsp. salt
1 lb. medium shrimp, cooked and
  peeled

1 pt. box cherry tomatoes
1 (6 oz.) can black olives, drained
1 (8 oz.) can water chestnuts,
  drained
1 (6 oz.) can whole mushrooms,
  drained
½ head cauliflower florets

Combine first 6 ingredients; mix well. In a large bowl, combine remaining ingredients, excluding cauliflower. Pour mayonnaise sauce over shrimp and vegetables, refrigerate. Before serving, add cauliflower florets. A TRUE EPICUREAN TREASURE!!

Mary Sharp Rayner, Oxford, Mississippi

MISSISSIPPI NOTABLE:
William Faulkner lived most of his life in North Mississippi and much of his adult life in Oxford. Many critics consider him to be the greatest American novelist. Faulkner wrote of the people and places of Mississippi, and his novels and short stories relate man's possibilities of overcoming his own errors, and Faulkner's belief that man would not only endure but also prevail. In 1950, Faulkner was awarded the Nobel Prize for Literature.

MACARONI — SHRIMP SALAD

5 cups water
1½ lbs. fresh shrimp, unpeeled
4 cups corkscrew macaroni,
  uncooked
1 (10 oz.) pkg. frozen peas
½ cup sliced water chestnuts,
  drained

½-1 cup mayonnaise
2 Tbsps. parsley, chopped
1½ Tbsp. pimento, chopped
Dash of salt
Dash of pepper

Bring water to boil; add shrimp, and cook for 3 to 5 minutes. Drain well, and rinse with cold water. Chill; then, peel, and clean the shrimp; set aside. Cook macaroni according to package's directions. Drain, rinse with cold water, and drain again. Cook peas according to package's instructions, and drain. Combine shrimp, macaroni, peas, and remaining ingredients in a large bowl, toss until coated, and chill overnight. Delicious and pretty too!! *Serves 6.*

Kicker Hull, Jackson, Mississippi

REAL MISSISSIPPI FOLK'S FACT:
Real Mississippi folk can't pronounce "Chicago" but have no trouble with Kosciusko, Escatawpa, and Tchoutachouffe!

WEST INDIES SALAD

1 lb. lump crab meat	3 ozs. cider vinegar
4 ozs. Wesson oil	4 ozs. iced water
1 onion, chopped (Do not use a food processor.)	Lots of salt and pepper

Combine well all ingredients, and place in a glass container. Set container in ice in refrigerator. Before serving, drain salad well. So pretty served on a bed of lettuce. Nice, easy, and good!!

Mary Jo Briggs, Jackson, Mississippi

SHRIMP MOUSSE

1 can cream of shrimp soup	1 onion, finely chopped
1 (8 oz.) pkg. cream cheese	1 cup mayonnaise
2 cans broken shrimp	Salt and pepper
1 envelope gelatin	

Warm soup, add cheese, and stir until cheese is melted. Mix in gelatin; add mayonnaise. Then, add shrimp, onion, salt and pepper. Pour mixture into a 5 cup mold that has been sprayed with Pam. Chill.

Kicker Hull, Jackson, Mississippi

BEST TOMATO ASPIC

3 cups V-8 Juice
2 envelopes Knox Gelatin
1 small onion, grated

½ tsp. Lea & Perrin
3 drops Tabasco

Heat 2 cups of the V-8, but do not boil. Grate onion into heated V-8. Pour remaining cup of V-8 over gelatin; stir well. Add gelatin mixture to warm V-8, and stir well. Pour into 6 custard cups, and refrigerate. THIS IS TRULY THE BEST!!

Margaret Lowery, Jackson, Mississippi

TOO GOOD TOMATO SPREAD SALAD MOLD

3 (3 oz.) pkgs. cream cheese
1 can tomato soup
2 Tbsps. gelatin
½ cup water
½ cup bell pepper, chopped

½ cup celery, chopped
½ cup onion, chopped
Several drops Tabasco (optional)
1 cup mayonnaise

Soften gelatin in the water, and melt cream cheese in the soup. Add gelatin; heat through. Cool; then, combine all the vegetables and mayonnaise with soup mixture, pour into a small mold, and refrigerate.
Serves 6.

Ruth Virden, Jackson, Mississippi

SUPER-N-EASY FRUIT SALAD

1 can Eagle Brand Milk
1 can cherry pie mix
1 small can crushed pineapple
¼ cup lemon juice
¼ tsp. almond extract
2 cups Cool Whip

Mix well in the order listed, and chill. SO GOOD!!
Serves 4-6.

Hattie Barnhill, Starkville, Mississippi

WINTER JEWEL SALAD

1 envelope plain gelatin
¼ cup cold water
1¼ cups hot water
2 Tbsps. sugar
1 tsp. salt
2 Tbsps. horseradish
2 Tbsps. vinegar
2 Tbsps. lemon juice
½ cup celery
½ cup beets
1 Tbsp. onion
½ cup cabbage, finely chopped

Soften gelatin in cold water, and dissolve in hot water. Add next 5 ingredients, and stir. Cool; when thick, fold in all the vegetables. Pour into individual molds or custard cups. Serve with mayonnaise (recipe, page 41) and on individual beds of lettuce.
Serves 4-6.

Maye Belle Bartlett, Como, Mississippi

TWENTY-FOUR HOUR SLAW

1 large cabbage, finely shredded
1 large onion (red or sweet), cut in
* rings*
¾ cup sugar plus 1 Tbsp.
1 cup vinegar

1 tsp. celery seed
1 tsp. prepared mustard
1 Tbsp. salt
1 cup salad oil

Combine cabbage and onion; sprinkle ¾ cup sugar on top. Bring to a boil remaining sugar and next 4 ingredients. While this mixture is hot, add salad oil. Pour hot mixture over cabbage mixture, and cover. Leave slaw in the refrigerator overnight.
Serves 6-8 generously.

FRESH BROCCOLI-CAULIFLOWER SALAD

1 onion, finely chopped
1 bunch fresh broccoli, chopped
1 bunch fresh cauliflower, chopped
1 cup mayonnaise

1 Tbsp. sugar
1 Tbsp. vinegar
Salt to taste

The broccoli and cauliflower should be chopped in ½ inch pieces. Combine all the ingredients, and refrigerate. This can be used as a salad or vegetable dish and is very good with ham or any grilled meat!!

Trudy Wiggins, Pascagoula, Mississippi

CHRISTMAS SALAD

1 small pkg. raspberry jello	1 (6 oz.) bottle Coca Cola
½ cup hot water	½ cup nuts, chopped
1 (8 oz.) can crushed pineapple, drained	1 (3 oz.) pkg. cream cheese, grated
1 (16 oz.) can cranberry sauce	Mayonnaise

In a mixing bowl, combine jello and water. Stir in pineapple; add cranberry sauce, mixing well. Next, add Coca Cola and nuts. With mayonnaise, grease a small (4 cup) mold; pour in jello mixture. Refrigerate until "set." Sprinkle with cheese before serving. So pretty, festive, and good!!
Serves 6-8.

Martha Ann McLaurin, Jackson, Mississippi

MISSISSIPPI FESTIVAL:

Christmas at Florewood, sponsored by Mississippi's Department of Natural Resources Bureau, is held at Florewood Plantation near Greenwood, Mississippi. Florewood is decorated with 1840's Christmas decorations, and there is a lovely evening candlelight tour of this beautiful plantation home. This tour, held in December, includes music and refreshments.

BEST HONEY-FRUIT SALAD DRESSING FOR FRESH FRUIT

2/3 cup sugar	1/3 cup honey
1 tsp. dry mustard	5 Tbsps. vinegar
1 tsp. paprika	1 Tbsp. lemon juice
1 tsp. salt	1 Tbsp. onion, grated
1 tsp. celery seed	1 cup oil

Mix dry ingredients together, and add honey, vinegar, lemon juice, and onion. Beat with a rotary beater or an electric mixer. Add oil gradually while beating. Chill thoroughly. Outstanding on fresh fruits!

Yields 2⅔ cups.

Ann Rushing, Product Production Specialist
Mississippi Home Extension,
Department of Agriculture and Commerce

MISSISSIPPI FESTIVAL:
The Neshoba County Fair, held in August in Philadelphia, Mississippi, is the only remaining campground fair in the United States and has been an annual event since 1889!

WATERMELON SALAD POT POURRI

2 ½ cups watermelon, diced and
 seeded
2 ½ cups water
1 ¾ cups sugar
½ cup fresh lemon juice (2-3 lemons)
1 tsp. almond extract

Watermelon juice
¼ cup fresh orange juice (one
 orange)
½ tsp. kirsch (optional)
Fresh fruit

Bring sugar and water to a boil; boil for 5 minutes. Set aside to cool.
Squeeze lemons for the juice. To cooled mixture, add lemon juice, almond
extract, watermelon cubes, and any watermelon juice. Put into a blender;
mix. Put mixture into a 2-quart ring mold, stir twice, and freeze. Remove
from mold; fill center with fresh fruit-strawberries, cantaloupe, pineapple,
honey dew, peaches, pears, kiwi, oranges, etc. Moisten salad with orange
juice and kirsch.

*"This salad is gorgeous and delicious! The mold, by itself, makes a pretty
fruit mold for fruit punches and/or cocktails that are served in large punch
bowls or containers."*

Jeanne Verlenden, GREAT FLAVORS OF MISSISSIPPI

MISSISSIPPI FESTIVAL:
Watermelon Festival in Mize, Mississippi, in July.

THREE BEAN SALAD IN MARINADE

2 cans Green Giant 3-Bean Salad,
  drained
1 bunch green onions, chopped
Plenty of black pepper

1 can medium pitted ripe olives,
  halved and drained
Wishbone Italian Salad Dressing
2 or 3 tomatoes, chopped

Mix 3-bean salad, onions, and olives with lots of pepper. Half cover with salad dressing. Refrigerate overnight; stir several times. An hour before serving, add tomatoes; let marinate.
Serves 6.

Gertrude Wiggins, Pascagoula, Mississippi

BEST HOMEMADE MAYONNAISE

4 egg yolks
2 cups Wesson oil
Juice of 1½ small lemons
1 Tbsp. (plus a little) olive oil

8 splashes Tabasco
1 heaping tsp. salt
1 Tbsp. boiling water

Several hours before making mayonnaise, place yolks, oil, juice, and olive oil in the refrigerator. Refrigerate a small electric mixer bowl (blender can be substituted) and beaters. Beat yolks at high speed until light and fluffy. Add oil, ¼ cup at a time, and beat between additions. Turn mixer down a bit, and add olive oil. Beating all the time, add Tabasco and salt. Lastly, add boiling water which keeps it from curdling. Refrigerate.
"This mayonnaise recipe will never fail if you follow the instructions to the letter!"

From the Recipes of Mrs. G. Garland Lyell, Jackson, Mississippi

PRIMOS RESTAURANT'S HOUSE DRESSING
(For Best Green Salad)

1 cup Wesson oil
1 cup white vinegar
2 cups cold water
½ tsp. salt
¼ tsp. sugar
¼ tsp. white pepper

1 medium onion, finely chopped
½ garlic head, finely chopped
Greek Feta cheese (optional)
Head of Iceberg or Romaine lettuce

Put onions and garlic in a cheese cloth in a stainless steel container. Add remaining ingredients excluding lettuce and cheese, and let marinate for 6 to 12 hours. Take dry, crisp greens, and cut into one inch squares. Put lettuce in a bowl, shake dressing, and pour needed amount over the greens. Toss greens in dressing, and use tongs or fingers to lift greens, shaking off any excess dressing. Serve on a chilled plate, and top with Greek Feta cheese. Any remaining dressing can be kept in the refrigerator for a week.

Primos Restaurant, Jackson, Mississippi

MISSISSIPPI FACT:
Primos is a very fine family owned restaurant that has offered continuous service to Mississippians, their guests, and visitors since 1929.

DELICIOUS HAM AND CHEESE SANDWICHES

1 stick butter (real)
2 Tbsps. mustard with horseradish
Grated onion to taste

2 Tbsps. poppy seeds
12 ham slices
12 Swiss cheese slices

Melt butter, and add mustard, onion, and poppy seeds, mixing all together well. With a pastry brush, spread butter mixture on both sides of either croissants or bread buns. Then, place a slice of ham, topped with a slice of cheese, on the croissant or bun. Wrap each sandwich in foil, and freeze. When ready to eat, place sandwiches on a cookie sheet, and heat for 30 minutes at 350°. SO GOOD!! The butter makes enough to spread about 10-12 sandwiches. For a change, substitute Monterey Jack cheese for the Swiss.

Laurie McRee, Mary Alice White
Jackson, Mississippi

REAL MISSISSIPPI FOLK'S FACT:

Real Mississippi folk would dig their own well before they drank Perrier!

GENUINE IMITATION REAL PIT BARBECUE

1 5-6 lb. pork roast, cheapest cut is
  perfect, allow ½ lb. per person
3 parts Kraft Hickory Flavored
  Barbecue Sauce

1 part Kraft Hot Barbecue Sauce

Wrap roast in foil, place in a large skillet, and bake at 225° for at least 12 hours. Drain off fat; shred the pork, removing any fat. Combine sauces; then, mix meat with enough sauce to moisten. Refrigerate, or freeze. Reheat meat before serving. Serve on warm buns with extra sauce and slaw (recipe, page 37). GREAT FOR A REAL MISSISSIPPI COOK-OUT!!

Lacey Morris, GREAT FLAVORS OF MISSISSIPPI

MISSISSIPPI FESTIVAL:

The National Tobacco Spitting Contest is held in Raleigh, Mississippi, in June. This is a world class contest which occurs at Billy John Crumpton's farm west of Raleigh. Other events include live entertainment and political speaking as well as wonderful food!!

MARVELOUS BEEFY CHEESE SANDWICH

1 (4 oz.) jar chipped beef
1 Tbsp. butter
1 lb. (2½ cups) tomatoes, drained

1 Tbsp. chili powder
1 lb. sharp Cheddar cheese, grated
3 eggs, slightly beaten

Saute beef in butter for 5 minutes. Add tomatoes and chili powder. Then, add cheese and eggs to beef mixture; stir until melted. Refrigerate. When ready to serve, spread beefy cheese mixture on 2 slices of your favorite bread. Close the sandwich; butter the outside. Then, cook as you would a grilled cheese sandwich. The beefy cheese mixture keeps well in the refrigerator for days!
Makes 6-8 sandwiches.

Montie Walker, Tribbett, Mississippi

MISSISSIPPI FACT:

Mississippi proudly claims to have produced more famous writers in proportion to its population than any other state! The rich history and folklore of Mississippi have been immortalized through the works of writers such as Eudora Welty, William Faulkner, Tennessee Williams, Richard Wright, Willie Morris, and many others.

THE MEXICAN CLUB SANDWICH

1-12 inch flour tortilla
2 Tbsps. guacamole spread (See below.)
1 Tbsp. green chilies, diced
½ cup lettuce, shredded
2 Tbsps. tomato, diced

2 strips bacon, cooked until crisp and well drained
2 ozs. turkey, thinly sliced
1 oz. Cheddar cheese, thinly sliced
3 large ripe olives, pitted

When spreading ingredients on the tortilla, keep food toward the front half in order to roll neatly. Spread guacamole on the flat tortilla, and sprinkle with chilies, lettuce, and tomato. Then, top with bacon and turkey. Fold in the sides of the tortilla (2 inches on each side), and roll up. Top with cheese, and melt under the broiler. Cut sandwich into 3 even pieces, securing each with a toothpick and the whole ripe olives. Makes 1 delectable serving!

GUACAMOLE SPREAD

1 ripe avocado, mashed
1 Tbsp. onion, minced
1 Tbsp. tomato, chopped

1 Tbsp. green chilies, diced
1 Tbsp. green chili Picante sauce
Juice of 1 lemon

Mix all the ingredients together well. Delicious! This is good alone or with doritos too!

Bill McCrillis, Jackson, Mississippi

BREADS

ADELAIDE'S SOUR CREAM ROLLS

2 cups self-rising flour　　　　　　*1 (8 oz.) carton sour cream*
2 sticks butter, softened

With a spoon, mix flour and butter into dough. Then, stir in sour cream.
Drop into greased, minature muffin tins. Bake at 425° for 10 minutes or
until lightly browned. Easy and delicious!!
Yields 30 marvelous rolls!

Marjorie Dixon, Vaughan, Mississippi

MISSISSIPPI FESTIVAL:

*Hobo Day, held at the Casey Jones Museum in Vaughan in September,
features authentic hobos telling stories along with other entertainment
and bowls of hobo stew for everyone!*

REFRIGERATOR SPOON ROLLS

1 pkg. dry yeast
2 cups warm water
¼ cup sugar
1 egg, slightly beaten

½ cup cooking oil
1 tsp. salt
4 cups self-rising flour

Dissolve yeast in warm water. Add remaining ingredients; beat until well mixed. Place dough in an air tight container, and store in the refrigerator. As needed, spoon into greased muffin tins, and bake at 400° for approximately 20 minutes. Remember that there is no rising time!

Hattie Barnhill, Starkville, Mississippi

MISSISSIPPI NOTABLE:

Nathan Bedford Forrest arrived in Mississippi when he was 13 years old and lived practically all of his adult life in Mississippi. When he was 40 years old, he enlisted in the Confederate Army as a private, and he ended the war as Lieutenant General N.B. Forrest. General William T. Sherman of the Union Army called General Forrest "the very devil." Forrest once said that the secret of his success as a general was to "get there first with the most men!"

PAN ROLLS

¾ cup sugar	2 eggs
¾ cup shortening	6-7 cups flour
1 cup boiling water	1 Tbsp. salt
2 pkgs. yeast (I use Red Star.)	1 tsp. baking powder
1 cup water	½ tsp. baking soda

Cream sugar and shortening; add boiling water. Dissolve yeast in a cup of tepid water. Add eggs, and then, combine all. Knead, roll into 1½-inch balls, and place in 2 greased 9-inch pans. Let rise for an hour and a half. Then, bake in a 400° oven for 20 minutes. SO WONDERFUL AND EASY!!

Carolyn McIntyre, Jackson, Mississippi

MISSISSIPPI FACT:

Jackson, as Mississippi's new state capital, grew slowly at first because it was not located on a major road. Thus, Mississippi encouraged settlers to come to Jackson by offering them very cheap land. To own some of this land, a man had only to promise to build "a neat log or frame house, not less than 30 feet in length, by November of 1831!"

ORANGE MUFFINS

½ cup butter
1 egg yolk
2 tsps. baking powder
¼ tsp. soda
¼ cup milk

½ cup sugar
2 cups flour less 2 Tbsps.
¼ tsp. salt
½ cup orange juice and 1 tsp.
    orange rind, grated

Cream butter and sugar. Add egg yolk. Sift dry ingredients; then, combine milk and juice. Combine with creamed mixture by alternating dry and liquid mixtures; mix well. Pour in greased muffin tins, and bake at 400° for 20 minutes.

Mrs. G. C. Ford, Greenwood, Mississippi

SOUR CREAM MUFFINS

1 cup sour cream
1 Tbsp. cooking oil (to grease
    muffin tins)
1 1/3 cup flour
2 tsps. baking powder

2 Tbsps. sugar
1 egg yolk, beaten
½ tsp. soda
½ tsp. salt
1 egg white, beaten

Mix cream, sugar, and salt; add egg yolk, and blend together. Sift flour; measure, and then, add soda and baking powder, and sift again. Add to cream mixture, and fold in egg white. Bake in greased muffin tins at 350°. *Yields 12 muffins.*

Mrs. C. A. Davis, Natchez, Mississippi

APPLE SPICE BREAD

1 1/3 cup all-purpose flour
¾ tsp. soda
½ tsp. salt
1 tsp. ground cinnamon
½ tsp. ground cloves
1 cup plus 1 tsp. sugar

½ cup oil
2 eggs, beaten
1 tsp. vanilla extract
2 cups apples, coarsely chopped
½ cup raisins

Preheat oven to 350°. Mix flour, soda, salt, cinnamon, and cloves; set aside. Mix cup of sugar with oil in large bowl. Add eggs and vanilla; then, stir in apples and raisins. Add flour mixture; stir until well mixed. Grease a 1-quart bread pan; then line the bottom of the pan with waxed paper. Pour batter into the pan, smooth, and bake for 50 to 60 minutes at 350°. After bread has baked for 20 minutes, sprinkle top with teaspoon of sugar. Return to oven, and finish baking. Let cool before slicing. Wonderful!!

Martha Morris, Jackson, Mississippi

MISSISSIPPI FACT.

Since World War II, a number of Mississippi writers have won the Pulitzer Prize. Hodding Carter, Ira Harkey, and Hazel Brannon Smith have won in journalism, William Faulkner and Eudora Welty in fiction, Tennessee Williams in drama, and David Donald in biography.

CRANBERRY BREAD

2 cups flour
1½ tsps. baking powder
1 cup sugar
½ tsp. salt
½ tsp. baking soda
1 egg, beaten

1 large orange, juice and grated rind
2 Tbsps. butter, melted
2/3 cup boiling water
1 cup, pecans, broken
1 cup cranberries, finely cut

Sift together first 5 ingredients; add egg. Then, add remaining ingredients. Line a loaf pan with waxed paper; pour in bread mixture, and bake at 350° for an hour. Store for 24 hours before slicing. Keeps well, delicious, and easy.

Mrs. E. P. Cox, Columbus, Mississippi

BEST BEER BREAD

3 cups self-rising flour
3 Tbsps. sugar
1 Tbsp. dill weed

1 can beer, stale (left out and opened for 2-3 hours)
1/3 stick margarine, melted

Mix well first 3 ingredients; add stale beer, and pour batter into a greased bread loaf pan. Pour margarine over top of batter; bake at 350° for 50 minutes.

Beer Bread's dry ingredients in a quart zip-lock bag, tied with a festive ribbon, and the can of beer, attached to the bag with another festive ribbon, make a fun Christmas Happy!

CHAN PATTERSON'S MONKEY BREAD COFFEE CAKE

3 cans Pillsbury flaky biscuits   *2 cups sugar*
2 tsps. cinnamon   *2 sticks margarine, melted*

Tear each biscuit into thirds, roll each into a ball, and place in a bag which contains a cup of sugar that has been mixed with the cinnamon; shake biscuit pieces well in mixture. Put sugar coated biscuits in a Bundt pan that has been sprayed well with Pam. Then, mix remaining sugar with the margarine, and pour mixture over the balls of dough. Bake at 350⁰ for 30 to 40 minutes or until brown. Then, cool for 10 minutes, and turn out of Bundt pan. So easy and absolutely mouth-watering!!

Chan Patterson, Jackson, Mississippi

Chan Patterson teaches many cooking classes in the kitchen of the EVERYDAY GOURMET, a culinary shop, in Jackson.

MISSISSIPPI FACT:
Jackson, Mississippi's state capital, is located on LeFleur's Bluff which rises above the Pearl River. The city is named in honor of "Old Hickory," Andrew Jackson, the seventh President of the United States.

DELICIOUS COFFEE CAKE

1 box Duncan Hines White Cake
 Mix
½ cup sugar
¾ cup oil
1 cup sour cream
4 eggs
2 tsps. cinnamon

3 Tbsps. sugar (brown or white)
½ cup nuts, chopped
FOR MARVELOUS GLAZE:
½ cup confectioner's sugar
2 Tbsps. milk
½ tsp. vanilla

Combine first 5 ingredients, adding eggs one at a time. Pour equal amounts of this mixture into 2 8-inch square pans. Mix together well the next 3 ingredients; then, top, in equal amounts, both cake batters (in squared pans). Bake for 25 minutes at 350⁰. While cakes are cooking, make Marvelous Glaze by mixing sugar, milk, and vanilla together. When cakes have finished baking, coat top of each cake with glaze. QUITE SIMPLY DELICIOUS!!

Susan Mims, Jackson, Mississippi

REAL MISSISSIPPI FOLK'S FACT:
Real Mississippi folk know that the North is anything on the other side of Memphis!

SOUR CREAM COFFEE CAKE

½ cup shortening
¾ cup sugar
1 tsp. vanilla
3 eggs

2 cups flour
1 tsp. baking powder
1 tsp. baking soda
½ pt. sour cream

Cream shortening, sugar, and vanilla. Add eggs one at a time; beat well after each addition. Sift together the dry ingredients; add to creamed mixture, alternating with sour cream and blending well after each addition. Set aside while making Pecan Topping.

PECAN TOPPING

4 Tbsps. margarine
¾ cup sugar

1½ tsps. cinnamon
½ cup pecans, chopped

Mix all ingredients together well. In a greased mini-Bundt pan, put a small amount of topping in the bottom of the pan. Add half the cake batter, then follow by sprinkling in remaining topping. Pour the rest of the batter over the topping. (Use a spatula to spread batter each time.) Bake for 50 minutes in a 350° oven. Cool on a rack for 10 minutes before removing from the pan.

Linda Scarborough, Columbus, Mississippi

SOUTHERN FRIED COFFEE·CAKES

1 cup sugar
2 eggs
1 tsp. baking soda
1 cup sour milk

1 tsp. nutmeg
Pinch of salt
1 (level) tsp. baking powder
2½ cups flour

Combine sugar and eggs; then, dissolve soda in sour milk, and add to sugar mixture. Mix well. Combine nutmeg, salt, baking powder, and flour; sift together. Fold flour mixture into sour milk mixture, and beat until dough is smooth. On a floured board, roll out dough to ½-¾" thickness. Cut with a doughnut or round cookie cutter, and fry in hot oil in a deep fat fryer or deep, heavy skillet (hot oil must completely cover each cake) until cakes are crispy brown. These cakes are wonderful hot or cold. If they are served cold, put powdered sugar in a brown bag, and gently shake cakes (2 or 3 at a time) in the bag to coat. Absolutely mouth watering!

GREAT FLAVORS OF MISSISSIPPI

MISSISSIPPI FACT:
During the Siege of Vicksburg, the Confederate and Union soldiers did not spend all their time fighting. They declared "unofficial truces" so that each side could pick blackberries and other edible wild fruit. Before long, hundreds of soldiers from both sides were meeting between the lines, discussing such things as the weather, girlfriends, and mistakes of their officers!!

DELTA SKILLET CORN BREAD

1½ cups corn meal
1 egg
1 cup buttermilk
1 cup sweet milk

½ tsp. salt
½ tsp. baking soda
3 Tbsps. shortening or bacon
   drippings

In a medium sized bowl, combine the first 6 ingredients; beat well. Heat fat or drippings in an 8-inch skillet, add to batter, and beat well. Pour batter into warm skillet, and bake for 30 minutes at 400°. Butter well, and serve. DELICIOUS!!

INDIAN CORN BREAD

6 fresh ears of corn
½ cup flour

Pinch of salt
4 Tbsps. fat (for skillet)

Cut corn off cob; scrape cob to get all the juice out. Mix corn, flour, and salt together; add all of the corn juice (and a little water if needed). Pour mixture into greased iron skillet; bake until done.

From the Recipes of the Choctaw Indian Tribe
Philadelphia, Mississippi

MISSISSIPPI FESTIVAL:
The Choctaw Indian Fair, in Philadelphia in July, features demonstrations of native arts, crafts, and dancing along with stickball, archery, blow gun, and rabbit stick competition. Native foods are prepared and served at the reservation.

HUSHPUPPIES A LA CROSS

3 cups self-rising corn meal
1 cup self-rising flour
1 large bell pepper, chopped

2 large onions, chopped
1 egg
1½ cups milk

Mix egg, bell pepper, and onion in a bowl; add meal and flour. Stir mixture, and slowly add milk until reaching desired consistency. Using index finger, slide mixture from a teaspoon into deep fat over medium flame, and cook until golden brown. ABSOLUTELY PEERLESS HUSHPUPPIES!! Yields 4 dozen.

Billy Joe Cross, Jackson, Mississippi

MISSISSIPPI BISCUITS

2½ cups flour
¾ tsp. salt
1 pkg. yeast
6 Tbsps. Crisco

4 Tbsps. sugar
½ tsp. baking soda
1 cup buttermilk, lukewarm

Dissolve yeast in buttermilk. Sift flour, salt, sugar, and soda together; cut in Crisco until batter looks like corn meal. Add buttermilk mixture to flour; knead for about 25 to 30 strokes. Roll out to about a half inch thickness. Cut, and dip in butter; place in pan in layers of 2. Let biscuits rise about 1½ hours; then, bake at 400° for about 12 minutes.

Mrs. Albert D. Duncan, Pontotoc, Mississippi

MISSISSIPPI SPOON BREAD

1 cup corn meal
1 2/3 cups boiling water
1 Tbsp. sugar
1 Tbsp. baking powder
1 tsp. salt

¼ cup butter
1 1/3 cups milk
3 egg yolks, well beaten
3 egg whites, stiffly beaten

In a saucepan, add boiling water to corn meal; cook, stirring until mixture is consistency of mush. Remove mixture from heat, and add next 4 ingredients. Stir in milk and yolks; fold in egg whites. Pour into a greased 2-quart casserole; cook at 325⁰ for 50 to 55 minutes. Eat hot, and enjoy!!
Serves 8.

LYNNE SMART'S NICE-N-EASY FRENCH BREAD

1 loaf French bread
2 sticks butter
1 tsp. salt or more (to taste)

1 Tbsp. poppy seeds or sesame seeds

With an electric mixer, whip butter, salt, and poppy seeds. Check mixture to be sure there is a salty taste for the secret to this recipe is the salty taste! Slice bread twice lengthwise; then, slice widthwise for bite sized slices. Spread butter mixture in between slices; ice with mixture on outside. Bake at 400⁰ for 15 minutes or until crispy and brown.
Serves 8.

Jeanne Verlenden, GREAT FLAVORS OF MISSISSIPPI

CHEESE BISCUITS

2 cups flour
½ tsp. salt
4 Tbsps. shortening
2/3 cup sweet milk

4 tsps. baking powder
¼ tsp. paprika
2/3 cup cheese, grated
2 tsps. prepared mustard

Mix dry ingredients, and sift. Cut in shortening; add cheese, milk, and mustard. Work in lightly with a fork. Toss on floured board, pat, and roll until ½" thick; cut with a small cutter. Bake at 450° for 12-15 minutes. SO GOOD!!

Mrs. John Liles, II, Grenada, Mississippi

JACKSON POPOVERS

4 eggs
1 cup milk
1 Tbsp. butter, melted

1 cup flour
1 tsp. sugar
1 tsp. salt

In a small bowl, beat eggs until fluffy. Add milk and butter, mixing well. Combine dry ingredients; add to egg mixture, and beat until smooth. Butter, generously, 6 custard cups. Set empty cups on a jelly roll pan, and place in a 400° oven for 5 minutes; remove from oven, and spoon an equal amount of batter into each cup. Bake at 400° for 25 minutes; reduce heat to 350°, and bake 25 minutes more. Turn off heat, and allow popovers to stand in the oven for 5 to 10 minutes. Serve hot with butter. OUTSTANDING! *Yields 6 wonderful popovers.*

St. James Episcopal Church Cooking School, Jackson, Mississippi

BANANA NUT LOAF

½ cup butter or margarine
2 whole eggs
1 tsp. baking soda
Pinch of salt
1 cup sugar

2 cups flour
3 bananas, mashed and whipped
3 cups nuts, finely chopped and
   sprinkled with flour

Cream butter, sugar, and eggs together. Add flour, soda, and salt. Then, add bananas and nuts. Bake in a greased loaf pan at 300° for about an hour. DELICIOUS!!

Mrs. J. L. Klaus, Sr., Macon, Mississippi
MISSISSIPPI DAR COOKBOOK

MISSISSIPPI FACT:
The Natchez Trace, which has been a major trail for over 8,000 years, extends from Nashville, Tennessee, to Natchez, Mississippi, with rich vegetation, a multitude of picnic areas, nature trails, historic markers, and state parks interspersed along the way to make the trip both enjoyable and interesting. Today the trace is a National Parkway and is maintained by the National Park Service.

VEGETABLES
AND
SIDE DISHES

NANCY'S MUSTARD SAUCE FOR STEAMED VEGETABLES

¾ cup mayonnaise
3 Tbsps. fresh lemon juice

1½ Tbsp. Dijon Mustard
½ cup heavy cream, whipped

Mix well first 3 ingredients; then, fold in whipped cream. Pour over steamed vegetables of your choice, and serve immediately. This sauce is wonderful on broccoli, asparagus, and green beans!!

Nancy Landrum, Columbus, Mississippi

ALFRED'S FAVORITE VEGETABLES

1 (20 oz.) pkg. frozen mixed
vegetables
½ cup celery, chopped
½ cup onions, chopped
1 cup Cheddar cheese, grated

½ cup mayonnaise
Salt and pepper to taste
½-¾ cup butter, melted
Pepperidge Farm Cornbread
Stuffing

Cook frozen vegetables per package's instructions; drain thoroughly. Mix with hot vegetables the next 5 ingredients. Combine butter and stuffing. Place vegetable mixture in a 1½-quart casserole, and top generously with stuffing-butter mixture. Bake at 375° for 20 to 25 minutes.
Serves 6-8.

Mary Hopton, Jackson, Mississippi

ARTICHOKE HEART CASSEROLE

1 (14 oz.) can artichoke hearts	2 cups, thick, rich white
1 (16 oz.) can tiny, whole boiled	sauce (recipe, page 76)
onions	Salt and pepper
4 eggs, hard boiled and sliced	Paprika
1 (8 oz.) stick sharp Cheddar	½ cup cracker crumbs
cheese	1 stick butter

In a 2-quart casserole, layer ingredients twice as follows: artichoke hearts, onions, eggs, cheese. Save a little cheese for the top. Cover layered ingredients with white sauce, then, salt, pepper, and paprika. Sprinkle top with cracker crumbs, dot generously with butter, and top with remaining cheese. Heat thoroughly in a 350⁰ oven.
Serves 6-8 generously.

Barbara Fullington, Yazoo City, Mississippi

MISSISSIPPI NOTABLE:
Author Willie Morris, born in 1934, spent his formative years in Yazoo City. His novel, GOOD OLD BOY, is about the mischief and magic of growing up in Yazoo City. His other works include NORTH TOWARD HOME and THE LAST OF THE SOUTHERN GIRLS. Mr. Morris now lives in Oxford, Mississippi, home of the University of Mississippi, where he teaches.

ARTICHOKE PIE

1 (14 oz.) can artichoke hearts
½ stick butter
½ cup onion, chopped
1 Tbsp. flour
½ cup half and half
4 eggs, beaten
½ cup sour cream
Salt, pepper, and nutmeg to taste

1 Tbsp. parsley, chopped
1 (9-in.) deep dish pie shell,
  unbaked (recipe, page 150)
½ cup Swiss cheese or Monterey
  Jack, shredded
¼ cup Cheddar cheese, shredded
¼ cup Parmesan cheese, grated

Preheat oven to 350⁰. Drain, and chop artichokes. Saute onions in butter
until tender; then, blend in flour. Gradually, add half and half; cook over
low heat until thick. In a bowl, combine eggs, sour cream, seasonings, and
parsley. Add onion mixture to egg mixture. Place artichokes on the
bottom of the pie shell, sprinkle with cheeses, and pour egg mixture over
top. Bake for 45 minutes or until set. Let stand 5 minutes before serving.
Delicious served hot or cold!!
Serves 6.

Jane Winston, Jackson, Mississippi

MISSISSIPPI FACT:
*The Choctaw game of stickball, famous in Mississippi, is the forerunner of
the modern game of lacrosse, a popular European and North American
sport.*

HOPPING JOHN

6 bacon slices, diced
2 (#2) cans Collinswood black-eyed peas
½ medium onion, chopped
¾ cup Mississippi long-grained rice, washed

2 cups boiling water
1 tsp. salt
Dash of sugar

Slowly fry bacon with onion. Cook rice in salted water until almost tender, and drain away any excess water. Add peas, bacon and onion mixture, and sugar to rice. Mix together well. Then, cover, and simmer over very low heat for approximately 20 minutes.

Compliments of the Mississippi Marketing Council
Jackson, Mississippi

MISSISSIPPI FESTIVAL:

The Chimneyville Crafts Festival, sponsored by the Craftsmen's Guild of Mississippi, is held at Jackson's Trade Mart in December. This wonderful festival features music, dramatic arts demonstrations, crafts demonstrations, and workshops.

SMOTHERED CABBAGE

1 medium cabbage
½ cup green pepper, finely chopped
¼ cup onion, finely chopped
¼ cup butter, melted
¼ cup all purpose flour
2 cups milk

½ tsp. salt
⅛ tsp. pepper
½ cup mayonnaise
¾ cup medium Cheddar cheese, shredded
3 Tbsps. chili sauce

Cut cabbage into wedges, removing core. Cover, and cook for 10 minutes in a small amount of slightly salted boiling water; drain well. Place wedges in a 13x9x2-inch dish; set aside. Saute green pepper and onion in butter until vegetables are tender. Add flour, and cook 1 minute, stirring constantly. Gradually add milk; cook over medium heat, stirring constantly until thickened and bubbly. Then, stir in salt and pepper, and pour mixture over cabbage. Bake at 375° for 20 minutes. While cabbage is baking, combine mayonnaise, cheese, and chili sauce; mix well. When casserole comes out of the oven, spoon cheese mixture over cabbage wedges, and bake for 5 minutes more.
Serves 8.

Susan Pratt, Jackson, Mississippi

MISSISSIPPI FACT:
Mississippi's state flower is the beautiful, sweet smelling magnolia.

CARROT FRITTERS

1 lb. carrots
2 eggs
¼ cup sugar
¼ tsp. salt

½ cup flour
2 tsps. baking powder
Powdered sugar (optional)

Clean, pare, and cook carrots; drain well, and mash. Beat in eggs; add sugar and salt. Sift flour and baking powder together. Stir into carrot mixture, deep fry; drain. Sprinkle with powdered sugar. SUPER!

Bill Clinton, Laurel, Mississippi

TRILBY'S CARROT CASSEROLE

6 bags carrots, cleaned, scraped,
and chopped
2 sticks butter

Salt and pepper to taste
1 tsp. nutmeg
1 lb. Cheddar cheese, grated

Boil carrots until tender. Mash with butter, salt, and pepper. Add nutmeg; mix in half the cheese. Put remaining cheese on top. Bake at 350° until top is golden brown and bubbly. Easily halved. ALL MEN LOVE!
Serves 20.

Trilby's Restaurant, Ocean Springs, Mississippi

MISSISSIPPI FESTIVAL:
The Landing of d'Iberville, held in Ocean Springs the last weekend in April, features a costumed dramatization of the 1699 landing, an arts and crafts show, a street fair, parade, and ball.

CORN-N-RICE CASSEROLE

1 pkg. yellow rice
1 can cream of chicken or cream of
  mushroom soup, undiluted

1 (12 oz.) can Mexicorn
1 cup cheese, grated

Cook rice according to package's directions. Add soup and Mexicorn. Spray a 1½-quart casserole with Pam, put soup mixture in the dish, and top with cheese. Bake, uncovered, at 350° for 20 to 30 minutes. A delightfully different way to enjoy corn!
Serves 4 generously.

TRUDY'S BROCCOLI CASSEROLE

1 (20 oz.) bag frozen broccoli
2 cups rice, cooked
1 onion, chopped

1 (16 oz.) jar Cheese Whiz
1 can cream of mushroom soup
1 can cream of chicken soup

In a saucepan, cook broccoli and onion until almost done. Remove from heat, and stir in soups and cheese. Stir in cooked rice, put mixture into a large, shallow baking dish; bake, uncovered, at 350° until casserole is set (about 30 minutes).
Serves 12 generously.

Gertrude Wiggins, Pascagoula, Mississippi

GRAM'S OLD FASHIONED CORN PUDDING

2 eggs, lightly beaten	Pinch of salt
2 Tbsps. sugar	1 (#2) can cream style corn
1 Tbsp. cornstarch	3 Tbsps. butter
1 cup milk	Nutmeg

To the eggs, add cornstarch, sugar, milk, salt, and corn; mix. Pour mixture into a casserole, dot with butter, and sprinkle with nutmeg. Set casserole in a pan of hot water, and bake at 300° for about 30 minutes. Gently stir pudding toward the center, and sprinkle again with nutmeg. Continue baking for another hour.

"This wonderful recipe of my grandmother's is one of my favorites. It is now in my collection as a newspaper clipping from the Memphis newspaper, THE COMMERCIAL APPEAL, and is dated May 6, 1955."

Lacey Morris, GREAT FLAVORS OF MISSISSIPPI

MISSISSIPPI NOTABLE:
Eudora Welty is considered by many to be the greatest living writer of Southern fiction. Miss Welty was born in 1909 in Jackson where she still resides. As her knowledge and love of Mississippi grew, she began to write short stories and novels about Mississippians and their history. These novels and short stories cover all sections of the state, from South Mississippi to the Delta to Northeast Mississippi's hill country.

EGGPLANT WITH SHRIMP CASSEROLE

4 qts. eggplant, cubed and soaked
   in water and salt
2 cups water
1 cup sauterne
2 Tbsps. oil
2 cups onion, chopped
1 cup bell pepper, chopped
1 clove garlic, minced
¼ cup fresh parsley

2 dashes garlic powder
1 tsp. onion salt
1 tsp. celery salt
1 tsp. hot sauce
1 Tbsp. soy sauce
2 Tbsps. Worcestershire sauce
2 eggs, beaten
1½ cups shrimp, cooked and peeled
Bread crumbs

Soak eggplant in salted water for an hour. Drain, and rinse. In a large saucepan, combine eggplant, water, and sauterne; cook until tender. In a separate saucepan, heat oil, and saute onion, bell pepper, garlic, parsley, and dash of garlic powder. Next, drain and mash eggplant, reserving liquid to be added later if needed. Add onion and green pepper mixture to eggplant. Then, add another dash of garlic powder, onion and celery salts, hot, soy, and Worcestershire sauces, and fold in eggs. Then, add shrimp. Put in a large, buttered casserole, and sprinkle bread crumps on top. Cook in a 350° oven for about an hour or until bread crumbs are brown, and casserole is bubbly. This is one of my family's favorites!!

Nancy Landrum, Columbus Mississippi

HOT FRUIT CASSEROLE

3 large oranges, unpeeled and
  sliced into quarters
1 (#2½) can pineapple
1 (#2½) can peaches
1 (#2½) can pears
1 stick butter, cut into small pieces

2/3 cup sugar
1/3 cup flour
Pinch of salt
¼ cup sherry
Brown sugar (optional)

Cook oranges in water until they are tender. Drain. Cut all fruit into chunks. Drain, and remember not to use any juices in the casserole. Into the top of a double boiler, put fruit. Sift sugar, flour, and salt together, and add to fruit. Then, add butter, and turn heat on low, stirring mixture until it is well blended. Continue to stir constantly until fruit is hot and mixture is completely blended. Then, remove from fire, and cool. Add sherry, and sprinkle with brown sugar. Before serving put in a moderate oven, and heat through. This may be made ahead of time and frozen. You may use any fruit you desire. A fine Mississippi dish!
Serves 6-8 generously.

Mrs. J. H. Hogue, Yazoo City, Mississippi
MISSISSIPPI DAR COOKBOOK

FRENCH STYLE GREEN BEAN-N-CORN CASSEROLE

1 (15½ oz.) can, French style green
  beans (Can use frozen.)
1 (12 oz.) can shoe peg white corn
1 can cream of celery soup
1 cup sour cream
1 cup sharp Cheddar cheese,
  grated

½ cup onion, chopped
1 cup water chestnuts, sliced
1 sleeve Ritz crackers, finely
  crushed
1 stick margarine, melted
Slivered almonds (optional)

Drain beans and corn, and spread in the bottom of a 9x13-inch pyrex pan. Mix next 5 ingredients together well, and spread on top of beans and corn. Mix cracker crumbs in margarine, and spread over top of casserole. Sprinkle generously with almonds. Bake at 350° for 30 to 45 minutes or until bubbly in the center. Easy and good!!
Serves 9-10.

Ruthie Owen, Jackson, Mississippi

MISSISSIPPI FACT:
With the ingenuity typical of Mississippians, the commodities shortages caused by the Civil War were solved by making coffee from parched corn, okra, or sweet potatoes, and tea from dried raspberry leaves. Tree bark and berries furnished inks and dyes, and plaited cornshucks made horse collars!

MISSISSIPPI GREENS

2 bunches greens (turnip, mustard,
  or collard), washed and "grit" free
Salt to taste
1-1 1/2 cups water
2 hot red peppers

1/2 tsp. black pepper
Pinch of sugar
1 ham hock or bacon strip
Vinegar to taste

In a Dutch oven, add salt, hot peppers, and meat to water, and bring to boil. Let simmer about 10 minutes. Then, add greens, black pepper, and sugar. Cook over low heat for about 45 minutes to an hour or until greens are tender and with a little liquid remaining (Mississippi folks call this liquid "pot likker" which is great for serving with hot cornbread!). Season with vinegar just before serving. DELICIOUS! A TRULY SOUTHERN RECIPE FOR ALL KINDS OF GREENS!!

Serves 6-8.

Laurin Stamm, Food Editor
VICKSBURG EVENING POST
Vicksburg, Mississippi

MISSISSIPPI FACT:
The Yazoo-Mississippi Delta, which most Mississippians call simply, "the Delta," is an almost perfectly flat basin of the richest soil in the world. "The Delta's" most famous description is by writer, David Cohn, of Greenville, Mississippi. He describes it as "beginning in the lobby of the Peabody Hotel in Memphis and ending on Catfish Row in Vicksburg."

VERMICELLI AND CHEESE

1 (8 oz.) pkg. vermicelli

2 cups white sauce (recipe below)

2 cups Cheddar cheese (mild or sharp), grated

Bread crumbs, buttered

Layer vermicelli, white sauce, and cheese two or three times in a greased 2-quart casserole. Top with bread crumbs, and cook for 25 to 30 minutes at 375°. Quite simply WONDERFUL!!

Serves 6.

"A super supper dish to prepare at the end of one of those too busy days."

Jane Gerber, Jackson, Mississippi

BASIC WHITE SAUCE

4 Tbsps. butter (no substitutes)

4 Tbsps. flour

2 cups milk

Salt and pepper to taste

Melt butter; add flour, salt, and pepper, stirring constantly. Remove from burner, and stir in milk. Return to burner; stir constantly until sauce is thick and smooth.

Yields 2 cups.

This sauce is good in any recipe that calls for a white sauce and can liven up recipes that don't call for one!!

GREAT FLAVORS OF MISSISSIPPI

MRS. MORRIS' DEVILED OYSTERS
(Oyster Dressing)

1 onion, chopped
1 cup celery, chopped
1 bunch parsley, chopped
2 sticks butter
3 dozen oysters, cut up
9 eggs, boiled and chopped
2 cups Progresso bread crumbs

3 eggs, beaten
Dash of red pepper
1 tsp. Worcestershire sauce
Dash of garlic salt
½ cup parsley, chopped
Butter

Saute onion, celery, and parsley in a stick of butter for 3 or 4 minutes. Cook oysters in the other stick of butter until oysters curl. Place bread crumbs and boiled eggs in a large mixing bowl, and add sauteed vegetables and cooked oysters. Next, add beaten eggs, season with salt, pepper, and Worcestershire, and mix all together well. Place mixture in a greased 9x13-inch casserole, dot with parsley and butter, and bake for 30 minutes at 350°.

"We always have this with our Christmas dinner for it is out of this world with turkey!"

Lacey Morris, GREAT FLAVORS OF MISSISSIPPI

MISSISSIPPI FESTIVAL:
Blessing of the Fleet, Shrimp Festival, and Fais Do Do in Biloxi, Mississippi, in June, includes the Coronation of the Shrimp Queen, parade of decorated boats, and the blessing of the fleet.

RUTH BLACK'S MARINATED VEGETABLES

¼ cup wine vinegar
¼ cup salad oil
½ cup mayonnaise
¼ tsp. salt
¼ tsp. garlic powder
1½ tsps. mustard
1 egg, hard boiled and grated
3 Tbsps. chives, chopped

2 (15½ oz.) cans whole green beans, drained
2 (15 oz.) cans Belgian carrots, drained
2 (14 oz.) cans artichoke hearts, drained
2 (14½ oz.) cans asparagus, drained

Mix together vinegar and oil; add mayonnaise, salt, garlic powder, and mustard; fold in egg and chives. In a 3-quart casserole, arrange vegetables, and then, cover with marinade. Let vegetables soak overnight. Super good, easy, pretty, colorful, and not boring looking!!

Judith Travis, Jackson, Mississippi

MISSISSIPPI FACT:
The Civil War caused the cost of commodities to skyrocket in Mississippi. In 1862 in Jackson, shoes were selling for $25 a pair, boots for $50 a pair, hats for $15 to $20 apiece, coffee for $4 a pound, tea for $25 a pound, salt for $75 to $100 per sack, and whiskey for $15 a gallon!

IANEOLIAN MANN'S HASH BROWN POTATO CASSEROLE

1 (32 oz.) pkg. hash brown frozen
  potatoes, thawed
1 cup butter, melted
1 cup cream of chicken soup,
  undiluted

12 ozs. American cheese, grated
1 (8 oz.) carton sour cream
1 tsp. salt
½ small onion, chopped
2 cups corn flakes, crushed

Place potatoes in a 9x13-inch baking dish. Mix together half a cup butter and next 5 ingredients; pour over potatoes. Top with corn flakes, and drizzle other half a cup butter over all. Bake at 350°, uncovered, for 45 minutes. TOO GOOD!!
Serves 12.

SWISS POTATO CASSEROLE

6 lbs. potatoes
2 (14 oz.) jars pimento, chopped
1 cup salad olives, chopped
2 bunches green onions, chopped

12 slices Swiss cheese, 8 slices cut
  in cubes
1¼ cups mayonnaise
Salt and pepper to taste

Cook potatoes until done, peel, and cut into chunks. Add pimento, olives, green onions, cubed cheese, and mayonnaise. Season with salt and pepper. Place in an oblong 2-quart casserole, top with remaining cheese slices, and bake, uncovered, at 350° for 30 minutes or until bubbly. WONDERFUL AND DIFFERENT!
Serves 12.

Jeanne Verlenden, GREAT FLAVORS OF MISSISSIPPI

MARVELOUS STUFFED POTATOES

6 potatoes, washed and baked 1
  hour at 450⁰
Salt and pepper to taste
2 sticks butter
½ cup green onions, chopped
¼ cup pimento, chopped
¾-1 large (12 oz.) can evaporated
  milk
1 cup (or more) Cheddar cheese,
  grated

Cut and scoop potato pulp out of cooked potatoes. Then, add remaining ingredients, and mix well with an electric mixer. Fill potato hulls with potato mixture. Sprinkle more cheese on top. (I sometimes bake an extra potato to have more pulp for the 12 hulls.)
Yields 12 stuffed hulls.

Jody Brown, Jackson, Mississippi

SOUTHERN TOMATO PIE

1 (9 in.) pie crust, cooked until it is
  light brown
2-3 good sized tomatoes
1 Tbsp. Italian seasoning or to
  taste
1 Tbsp. oregano or to taste
1½ tsps. chives or to taste
Salt and pepper to taste
1 cup sharp cheese, grated
1 cup mayonnaise

Sprinkle tomato slices with seasoning, oregano, chives, salt and pepper; place slices in pie crust. Combine cheese and mayonnaise to make a thick paste; then, cover tomatoes with paste. Bake at 350° until tomato paste is bubbly and the crust is a deep, golden brown.

SICILY'S RICE ALMONDINE

2 cups rice, uncooked
1 can mushroom soup
1 stick butter, melted

½ cup almonds
½ tsp. nutmeg
1 (4 oz.) can button mushrooms

Cook rice according to package's directions. Put a layer of rice in a buttered 9x13-inch (pan) casserole. Add half the soup, nutmeg, mushrooms, almonds, and butter. Repeat layering once again. Cook, covered, at 350° for 20 to 30 minutes or until thoroughly browned.

Sicily Morris, Jackson, Mississippi

FLORENTINE RICE QUICHE

1 egg, beaten
2 cups rice, cooked
2/3 cup Swiss cheese, grated
1 pkg. frozen chopped spinach
2 Tbsps. butter
3 eggs, beaten

1 Tbsp. salt
1 cup small curd cottage cheese
¼ cup Parmesan cheese, grated
6 Tbsps. cream
3 drops Tabasco

Combine rice, Swiss cheese, and 1 egg. Spread mixture into a greased quiche pan, and refrigerate. Cook spinach, and press out all liquid; cool, and add remaining ingredients. Pour spinach mixture over rice and cheese (quiche) crust. Bake for 30 to 35 minutes in a 350° oven or until firm. SCRUMPTIOUS!!

Nicki Griffing, Jackson, Mississippi

EASY-N-DELICIOUS SPINACH CASSEROLE

6 pkgs. frozen chopped spinach,
  drained
2 envelopes Lipton's Onion Soup
  Mix

2 cartons sour cream
1 roll Kraft Jalapeno cheese
Bread crumbs

Cook spinach according to package's directions. Combine sour cream, soup mix, and cheese; add to drained spinach. Pour into a 9x13-inch pyrex dish, and top with bread crumbs. Bake, covered, at 350° for 20 to 30 minutes (until heated through). Easily halved. SO GOOD!
Serves 12 generously.

Nancy Arrington, Meridian, Mississippi

MISSISSIPPI FACT AND FESTIVAL:
No trip to Mississippi would be complete without visiting Meridian's Jimmie Rogers Museum which honors the "Father of Country Music," a native of Meridian. In April, Meridian hosts the Lively Arts Festival which features professional entertainers and special shows in the historic Temple Theater along with the Youth Theater, Student Art Show, and Children's Art Awareness Day at the Meridian Museum of Art!

SPAGHETTI, BACON, AND EGGS

Spaghetti, enough for 1 serving
2 slices bacon
½ medium onion, chopped
1 oz. dry white wine (optional)
1 egg

⅛ cup Parmesan cheese
Dash parsley flakes
Pepper
Herbs (your choice)

While boiling spaghetti, chop bacon strips, and fry until lightly brown. Remove bacon, and saute onion in bacon grease until transparent. Return bacon to skillet, add wine, and simmer. If you use wine, let mixture sit. While spaghetti is cooking, put egg into a large bowl, and beat along with Parmesan cheese, parsley, and any other spices. When spaghetti is done, drain; add immediately to egg mixture. The hot spaghetti cooks the eggs! Mix in bacon and onion mixture; serve.
Serves 1 very generously.

"My Italian roommate taught me this. It's also called Spaghetti Alla Carbonnara. All the ingredients are given in "per person" units so multiply by the number of people that you want to serve, from one to fifty!"

Louis Montgomery, Jackson, Mississippi

AUNT ERNIE'S SQUASH CASSEROLE

3 lbs. squash
2 tsps. salt
1 onion, finely chopped
1 Tbsp. butter

2 Tbsps. flour
1 cup whipping cream
8 ozs. Velveeta cheese
Ritz cracker crumbs for topping

Cook first 3 ingredients in a skillet, drain well, and cool. In a medium sized pan over medium heat, make a white sauce by combining butter, flour, and whipping cream; then, add cheese to white sauce, mixing together well. Layer squash and sauce mixtures in a medium sized casserole, repeating several times. Top with Ritz cracker crumbs. Cook for 30 minutes at 350°. MOUTH-WATERING!!!!
Serves 6-8.

From the Recipes of Ernestine Simmons, Tupelo, Mississippi

MISSISSIPPI FACT:
Elvis Presley's birthplace is located in Tupelo. This childhood home of the "King of Rock-n-Roll" is open year round to visitors.

STUFFED YELLOW SPRING SQUASH

8 medium yellow squash
2 small onions, chopped
½ cup ham, cooked and chopped
1 Tbsp. butter
2 eggs, beaten
2 cups cracker crumbs
Salt and pepper to taste

Dash of Tabasco
Dash of Worcestershire sauce
Dash of garlic powder
2 tsps. sugar
Paprika
Butter

Split squash lengthwise. Scoop out insides of each squash, and cook in a skillet with onions, ham, butter, salt and pepper, both sauces, garlic powder, and sugar. When done, add cracker crumbs and eggs; mix. Scald squash shells for a few minutes in hot water. Then, fill individual shells with cooked squash mixture. Top each filled shell with additional cracker crumbs, paprika, and drip a little butter from a pastry brush. Bake in a pan which contains a few drops of water to keep shells from sticking, until heated through. Serve immediately.
Serves 16.

Old Southern Tea Room, Vicksburg, Mississippi

MISSISSIPPI FACT:
If you are traveling through Mississippi, Vicksburg is worth an extra day! Tourist treats include the Vicksburg National Military Park, Riverboat rides, Historic Tour Homes, the Cairo Museum, Biedenharn Candy Company, "Olde Tyme Melodrama," Waterways Experiment Station, and the list goes on and on!

BAKED SWEET POTATOES

4 sweet potatoes   Margarine or butter

Rub the skin of each potato with a thin coat of margarine or butter. Place on a baking sheet in a 350⁰ oven for an hour and a half. Serve with a pat of margarine or butter. Easy, nutritious, and good!

Mississippi Department of Agriculture and Commerce

SWEET POTATO PUDDING

3 cups raw sweet potatoes, grated   9 Tbsps. sugar
2 Tbsps. butter   ½ cup brandy
2 eggs, beaten well   1 tsp. nutmeg
1½ cups milk

To beaten eggs, add milk, sugar, butter, brandy, and nutmeg. Mix with potatoes. Pour into a buttered 1-quart baking dish; bake at 325⁰ for 45 minutes. This is a wonderful holiday or cold weather dish!
Serves 4-6.

Jeanne Verlenden, GREAT FLAVORS OF MISSISSIPPI

MISSISSIPPI FESTIVAL:
The Delta Blues Festival, held in Greenville, Mississippi, in September, features blues artists performing their distinctive music in a day long tribute to Blues Music.

SWEET POTATO PUFFS

4 medium sweet potatoes	Nutmeg to taste
1 egg	¼ cup sugar
1 Tbsp. butter	1/3 cup flour
Marshmallows	Corn flake meal

Boil potatoes until well done; drain well. Cream egg, butter, sugar, and flour; mix with potatoes. If potatoes are soft, add a little more flour, and cream well. Place in the refrigerator until chilled. Spoon mixture into small balls, using half of a marshmallow for the center. Roll each ball in corn flake meal; then, fry in deep fat until puffs are brown. Wonderful for holiday and special meals!
Yields about 15 medium sized balls.

Carol Waller, Jackson, Mississippi

Carol Waller is a former First Lady of Mississippi. Her husband, Bill, was Governor of Mississippi from 1972-76.

MISSISSIPPI FACT AND FESTIVAL:

Vardaman, Mississippi, is called the "Sweet Potato Capital of the World" and hosts the Sweet Potato Festival annually in November.

MILDRED BROWN'S BAKED APRICOTS

7 (#2) cans apricots, drained (There
   should be no liquid remaining.)
12 ozs. brown sugar

½ (12 oz.) box Ritz Crackers,
   crumbled
Butter

Grease a 9x13-inch baking dish with a tablespoon of butter. Coat both the bottom and sides. Arrange apricots in the dish, and cover with brown sugar. Top with crumbled crackers. Dot liberally with butter, and bake at 350° for 30 minutes. A wonderful brunch or holiday dish!

Sister Simmons, Jackson, Mississippi

FIG PRESERVES

36 figs
1½ cups sugar

1 Tbsp. water
1 slice lemon

Remove any stems from figs, combine all ingredients, and cook in a heavy saucepan until thick. Cool. This recipe is easily doubled, tripled, etc. *Yields 1 pint of marvelous preserves!*

Carolyn McIntyre, Jackson, Mississippi

REAL MISSISSIPPI FOLK'S FACT:
Real Mississippi folk are proud of William Faulkner but never got around to reading one of his books!

MEATS
AND
MAIN DISHES

AUNT MARTHA'S BEEF STROGANOFF

2-3 lbs. beef tenderloin tips or
round steak, cut into bite sized
pieces
⅛ tsp. onion salt or chopped
scallion

1 cup cream of mushroom soup
½ cup water
1 (8 oz.) can mushrooms
½ pt. sour cream
Curled egg noodles or rice

Brown beef pieces in small amount of oil. When meat is browned, season with salt, pepper, and onion. Add soup and water; simmer gently for 40 to 50 minutes or until meat is tender. Fold in mushrooms and sour cream; bring to serving temperature. If thinner gravy is desired, thin with dry, light red wine. Serve over hot noodles or rice.
Serves 4-6.

Susan Pratt, Jackson, Mississippi

CHEESEBURGER LOAF

1 (4 oz.) can evaporated milk
1½ lbs. ground beef (Chuck is best.)
½ cup cracker meal
1 egg
½ cup onion, chopped

½ tsp. salt
1 tsp. garlic salt
1 Tbsp. prepared mustard
1 cup cheese, grated

Combine all ingredients; mix well. Place in a 1-quart loaf pan, and bake for 50 to 55 minutes at 375°. Delicious, nutritious, and easy!!
Serves 4-6.

Lacey Morris, GREAT FLAVORS OF MISSISSIPPI

EASY, DELICIOUS CHILI

1 lb. ground beef
2 small onions, chopped
2 (8 oz.) cans tomato sauce
2 (15 oz.) cans kidney beans

2 Tbsp. chili powder
Dash of red pepper
Garlic salt to taste
Scant tsp. sugar (optional)

Cook beef and onions until meat is thoroughly browned. Drain well; then, add tomato sauce, chili powder, and garlic salt. Cook slowly on top of the stove over low burner heat for 1½ hours. Add the beans for the last 30 to 40 minutes of cooking time. Remember, while cooking chili to add water for liquid as needed! SO EASY AND SO GOOD!!
Serves 4-6.

Montie Walker, Tribbett, Mississippi

REAL MISSISSIPPI FOLK'S FACT:
Real Mississippi folk think a hot tub is for taking a bath!!

91

INTENTIONAL HASH

2½-3 lbs. boneless chuck or round
  roast
1 (14½ oz.) can beef broth
1 bunch green onions, tops and all,
  chopped

2 tsps. potato starch or flour,
  dissolved in water
2 Tbsps. sage
½ tsp. thyme
Salt and pepper

Buy leanest roast possible. In a 10-inch skillet with a lid, place roast and beef broth. Cover, and simmer until very tender, about 1 to 1½ hours. Remove meat to a platter, and de-fat; then, chop meat into small pieces. Thicken broth in skillet with potato starch (available in specialty stores). If unavailable, measure broth, and thicken with flour, about 1½ teaspoons per cup liquid (remember to dissolve flour in a little water, potato starch too). Stir well, making a very thin gravy. Now add chopped meat, onions, sage, and thyme. Simmer briefly, salt to taste, and continue to simmer for 30 to 40 minutes to develop flavor. Sprinkle generously with black pepper, and serve on hot, split cornbread (recipe, page 58).
Serves 6-8.

"Most hashes are made from leftovers. This recipe is for a deliberate, straighforward preparation of a hash from scratch. Hence, the designation, Intentional Hash!!"

Dr. Lewis Crouch, Jackson, Mississippi

5-6 lb. brisket
2 tsps. celery salt
2 tsps. onion salt
2 tsps. garlic salt

2 tsps. cracked pepper
3 ozs. liquid smoke
3 ozs. Worcestershire sauce

Place brisket on heavy duty foil. Pierce meat with a fork, and pour liquid smoke, and Worcestershire over it. Sprinkle meat with the salts and pepper. Wrap tightly, place in a pan with a tight fitting lid, and refrigerate overnight. Bake at 250° for 5-6 hours.
Serves 10-12.

Trudy Wiggins, Pascagoula, Mississippi

LACEY'S EASY "NO FAIL" ROAST

*Eye of round, Sirloin tip, or rump
roast*

*Garlic salt
Lemon-Pepper Marinade*

Place roast in a black, iron skillet; punch holes in the roast with a fork. Sprinkle, heavily, with garlic salt and marinade. Cook in preheated 500° oven for 5 minutes per pound. Turn oven off; leave roast in oven for an additional 2 hours. When done, roast will be pink in center. EXCELLENT! Serve with Stuffed Potatoes (recipe, page 80) and a green salad (recipe, page 42).

Jeanne Verlenden, GREAT FLAVORS OF MISSISSIPPI

SPICY BEEF-N-CHEESE NOODLE BAKE

1¼ lbs. ground beef
1 clove garlic, crushed
1 tsp. salt
Dash of pepper
1 tsp. sugar
1 (8 oz.) can tomato sauce
1 (10 oz.) can tomatoes and chili
   peppers (Rotel)
1 tsp. chili powder

¼ tsp. dried basil
6 scallions, chopped
1 (3 oz.) pkg. cream cheese
1 cup sour cream
½ cup of Cheddar cheese, grated
1 (5 oz.) pkg. noodles, cooked
   according to package's directions, drained

Brown meat, and pour off fat. Add garlic, salt, pepper, sugar, tomato sauce, Rotel, chili powder, and basil. Mix scallions with cream cheese and sour cream. In a 2-quart casserole, layer as follows: 1/3 noodles, 1/3 scallion mixture, 1/3 meat mixture; repeat layering twice. Bake at 350° for 20 minutes. Remove from oven, sprinkle Cheddar cheese on top, and return to oven until cheese has melted. This recipe is easily tripled, and freezes well. All members of the family will love!!
Serves 6-8.

Susan Mims, Jackson, Mississippi

MISSISSIPPI FACT:
The city of Jackson is one of four cities in the world chosen to host the International Ballet Competition every fourth year. The other cities are the U.S.S.R.'s Moscow, Helsinki, Finland, and Varna, Bulgaria.

WHISKEY BEEF STEW

2½ lbs. chuck roast, cut into cubes
3 Tbsps. margarine
2 Tbsps. brandy
3 Tbsps. flour
2 bouillon cubes
2 Tbsps. tomato paste
1½ cups burgundy
¾ cup dry sherry
¾ cup port

1 can beef bouillon
⅛ tsp. pepper
4 peppercorns
3 bay leaves
Pinch of thyme
1 clove garlic
1 (16 oz.) can white onions
1 (16 oz.) can button mushrooms, drained

In a large Dutch oven, brown beef cubes in margarine. Remove beef from oven, add brandy, and heat until a vapor rises; ignite brandy, and add beef. Remove beef again; stir in next 3 ingredients, blend, and add next 4 ingredients. Next, add beef, pepper, peppercorns, bay leaves, thyme, and garlic; turn off the heat, add onions and mushrooms. Cover, put in the refrigerator; let stew sit overnight. Heat (the next day) at 325° for 50 to 60 minutes. Serve over rice. SCRUMPTIOUS IN THE WINTER AND MEN LOVE!!

Serves 6-8.   Merry Montjoy, Bay St. Louis, Mississippi

MISSISSIPPI FACT:
Bay St. Louis is the home of the National Space Laboratory, a NASA center, which features an indoor and outdoor exhibit area and guided tours of the installation which includes the Space Shuttle Test Complex.

WINIFRED CHENEY'S VEAL SCALLOPS with WINE AND MUSHROOMS

2 Tbsps. butter
1 Tbsp. oil
10-12 veal scallops, dried on paper
  towels
1 tsp. dried green onion
½ cup dry white wine
1 can beef bouillon
1½ cups whipping cream

1 Tbsp. flour, dissolved in water
Salt and pepper to taste
½ lb. fresh mushrooms, washed and
  tips removed
2 Tbsps. butter
1 Tbsp. oil
Salt and pepper to taste
Parsley for garnish

Place butter and oil in a large, 10-12-inch skillet over moderately high heat. When butter foam has almost subsided, arrange half the veal in the skillet. Do not crowd. Saute veal on each side for 4 or 5 minutes, regulating heat so that fat is hot but not burning. The scallops should be lightly browned. Remove scallops and continue cooking, using more butter if needed. When all scallops are browned, pour wine and stock into skillet along with onion, and scrape up all cooked juices with a wooden spoon. Boil until liquid is reduced to about a half cup. Add cream and the flour, and boil for several minutes until cream is thickened slightly. Remove from heat. Saute mushrooms in butter and oil over medium heat for 4-5 minutes. Arrange scallops on a hot platter. Spoon cream and mushrooms over scallops, and surround with rice or mashed potatoes. Dot with parsley, and serve.
Serves 4.
"Quick and easy, this elegant dish may be prepared in 30 minutes or less!!"

From the Kitchen of Winifred Green Cheney, Jackson, Mississippi

ANOLA CHICKEN

2 cups chicken, cooked and
  chopped
1 pkg. Uncle Ben's Long Grain and
  Wild Rice or Uncle Ben's Wild
  Rice, cooked per package's
  directions
4½ ozs. pimentos
1 onion, finely chopped

1 cup mayonnaise
Lemon juice
Salt and pepper
1 can cream of celery soup
1 (10 oz.) pkg. frozen French Style
  Green Beans (Can use canned.)
1 can fried onion rings (optional)

Combine soup, mayonnaise, and lemon juice; add remaining ingredients.
Bake at 350⁰ for 25 to 30 minutes. If using onion rings, top casserole with
them for the last 5 minutes of cooking time. DECIDEDLY DELICIOUS!
Serves 6-8.

Trudy Wiggins, Pascagoula, Mississippi

OVEN SAGE CHICKEN

1 fryer, cut up
2/3 cup lemon juice
½-¾ cup mayonnaise

4 tsps. sage
Seasoned salt to taste
2 bay leaves

Place chicken in shallow, foil lined pan. Cover with lemon juice. Dot
chicken pieces with mayonnaise. Sprinkle chicken with 2 teaspoons sage,
and salt to taste; add bay leaves. Bake for 30 minutes in preheated 400°
oven; turn, and sprinkle with remaining sage and salt. Bake for another 30
minutes. (If fryer is small, check after 20 minutes.)
Serves 4.

Kittye Wright, Columbus, Mississippi

BRAD'S LEMON CHICKEN

4 split fryers
Olive oil
Lemon-Pepper seasoning

Garlic salt
Hickory chips (for the grill)

Bathe chicken halves in the oil, rubbing in well. Coat chicken heavily with lemon-pepper seasoning, and sprinkle with garlic salt. Build a fire at one end of a covered grill, and add hickory chips to coals, heating coils, or burner. Place chicken on grill at the opposite end. Do not place chicken directly oven fire. Cover, and cook for an hour and 15 minutes; no basting or additional sauce is required. Turn chicken over, and cook an additional hour and 15 minutes. Easy and good!

Donna Dye, Jackson, Mississippi

Donna says that her husband, Brad, Mississippi's current Lieutenant-Governor, is an excellent cook! His Lemon Chicken is one of her favorite recipes of his!

MISSISSIPPI FACT:
The Governor's Mansion in Jackson dates from 1842 and was designed to "avoid a profusion of ornaments and adhere to republican simplicity as best comporting with the dignity of the State."

CHICKEN AND DUMPLINGS

1 chicken (hen)	½ cup butter
1 onion, chopped	1 cup milk
3 qts. water	2 cups self-rising flour
1½ tsp. salt	1 egg
1 Tbsp. pepper	1 cup buttermilk

Combine first 5 ingredients in a Dutch oven. Simmer for an hour; remove chicken, cool, bone, and cut into pieces. Return chicken pieces to broth, stir in butter and milk, and bring to a boil. In a bowl, combine flour, egg, and buttermilk to make dough for dumplings. Knead dough 5 or 6 times. Roll dough to ⅛ inch thickness (I think that the secret to superb dumplings is rolling the dough as thin as possible.). Cut dough in strips that are 1 inch by 6 inches. Then, stretch dough with hands to break; drop dough in boiling broth, reduce heat, and cook for 5 to 10 minutes.
Serves 6.

Sicily Morris, Jackson, Mississippi

Delicious variations include adding either a can of mushroom or celery soup or both to the broth. The dumplings are excellent as "pea dumplings" which are made the same way using at least 1 cup of chicken broth and a (10 ounce) package of frozen peas and omitting the chicken. You can also include the peas when using chicken.

CHICKEN PAPRIKA

2 whole broiler/fryer chicken
  breasts, halved
2 broiler/fryer thighs
2 broiler/fryer drumsticks
1½ tsps. Accent
1/3 cup flour
1 tsp. salt
¼ tsp. pepper
1/3 cup corn oil

2 cans tomato soup
2 (4 oz.) cans sliced mushrooms,
  drained
½ cup water
½ cup onion, chopped
1 Tbsp. paprika
1 bay leaf
1 cup sour cream
Pasta (I use flat, egg noodles.)

Sprinkle chicken with Accent. Mix flour, salt, and pepper. Roll chicken in flour to coat. Heat oil over medium heat; brown chicken on all sides. Pour off excess fat; then, add soup, mushrooms, water, onion, paprika, and bay leaf, stirring all together. Simmer, covered, for 45 minutes or until a fork can be inserted into chicken with ease. While simmering, remember to stir now and then. Before serving, remove bay leaf, and blend in sour cream. Reheat for 2 to 3 minutes, and serve over noodles.
Serves 8.

Eloyse Pouncey, Gautier, Mississippi

Mrs. Pouncey's Chicken Paprika was Mississippi's Winner in the 1975 National Chicken Cooking Contest!!

MISSISSIPPI FESTIVAL:
Gautier is one of 11 Gulf Coast communities that participates in the Gulf Coast Pilgrimage, held annually, usually in April.

CHICKEN ROTEL

1 5-lb. hen, cooked and boned
2 onions, chopped
1 bell pepper, chopped
2 stalks celery, chopped
1 (7 oz.) pkg. vermicelli
1½ qts. chicken broth, saved from cooking hen
1½ sticks margarine
2 Tbsps. Worcestershire sauce
1 (10 oz.) can Rotel tomatoes with chilies
1 large can LeSeur English peas
1 (6 oz.) can mushrooms, drained
1 lb. Velveeta cheese, cut into small pieces
Salt and pepper

Saute onions, pepper, and celery in margarine. Cook vermicelli in chicken broth; add tomatoes and Worcestershire, and cook until thick, stirring frequently. Then, add peas and mushrooms. Stir in cheese pieces until completely melted. Combine vermicelli mixture with onions, pepper, and celery; mix in chicken pieces. Pour into 2 2-quart casseroles; heat until bubbly. Freezes well. This is delightful served with a green salad (recipe, page 42) and French bread (recipe, page 60).
Serves 16.

Mary Lane Nichols, Vaughan, Mississippi

MISSISSIPPI FACT:
The Casey Jones Museum in Vaughan commemorates the legendary railroad engineer, killed 1 mile north of the museum in 1900 and interprets the story of railroading in Mississippi.

CHICKEN TETRAZZINI

2 fryers, boiled and boned,
  reserving broth
3 onions, chopped
3 stalks celery, chopped
½ bell pepper, chopped
1 lb. vermicelli spaghetti

1 stick butter
1 lb. Velveeta cheese
2 cans cream of mushroom soup
½ (4 oz.) can pimento
Garlic salt to taste
Salt and pepper

Cook fryers in water with salt and pepper. After boning chicken, tear it into good sized pieces, and set chicken and stock aside. In half a cup stock, cook onion, celery, and bell pepper. Cook spaghetti in remaining stock. Add butter to spaghetti/stock mixture. Then, add cheese, mixing well; add soup, pimento, green pepper, onion, celery, chicken pieces, and garlic salt. Add some water if mixture is too thick. Place in a large casserole or 2-2 quart casseroles, cover, and heat for 40 to 45 minutes at 350⁰. SO GOOD! Recipe is easily halved.
Serves 12.

Sara Hinds, Tupelo, Mississippi

MISSISSIPPI FESTIVAL:
Gumtree Festival in Tupelo in May.

DENNERY'S CHICKEN ANGELO

1 8 oz. chicken breast
1 Tbsp. butter
½ cup mushrooms
1 tsp. scallions, chopped

½ tsp. garlic, minced
2 ozs. creamed sherry
1 artichoke, quartered
Salt and pepper

In a hot skillet, melt butter, add chicken, season to taste, and saute. When chicken is half done (about 20 minutes), turn, add scallions, mushrooms, and garlic, and continue to cook. When chicken is almost done, add sherry, reduce heat, and cook until sherry is absorbed. Add artichoke, and heat through. Serve immediately. EASY AND DELICIOUS! Recipe is easily doubled, etc.
Serves 1.

"Dennery's Restaurant is one of our favorite restaurants in Jackson, and we love the Chicken Angelo, for it is an elegant, special dish which is easy to prepare!"

Bill and Brenda Blackwell, Jackson, Mississippi

CRAB STUFFED CHICKEN BREASTS

4 whole chicken breasts or 8
   halves, boned and skinned
½ cup green onions, thinly sliced
¼ lb. fresh mushrooms, thinly
   sliced
¼ cup butter
3 Tbsps. flour
¼ tsp. thyme
½ cup chicken broth

½ cup milk
½ cup dry white wine
Salt and pepper to taste
8 ozs. crab meat or 1 (6½ oz.) can
   crab meat, drained
1/3 cup parsley, thinly sliced
1/3 cup dry bread crumbs, finely
   rolled
1 cup Swiss cheese, shredded

Pound breasts between waxed paper until they are ¼ inch thick. Saute onions and mushrooms in butter; then, stir in flour and thyme. Blend in broth, milk, and wine, cooking until thick. Season with salt and pepper. Stir together ¼ cup wine sauce with crab meat, parsley, and bread crumbs. Spoon equal amounts of mixture on each chicken breast. Roll up, and place seam side down in a greased 9x13-inch baking dish. Pour remaining sauce over chicken; sprinkle with Swiss cheese. Cover, and bake for an hour at 350⁰. This can be made a day ahead, and refrigerated. Save adding Swiss cheese until cooking time. DIVINE!!
Serves 8.

Jenny Foster, Jackson, Missisippi

MISSISSIPPI FACT:
Mississippi ranks sixth in poultry production in the United States.

GREEN CHICKEN ENCHILADAS

1 lb. bag fresh spinach
1 can chicken broth
1 clove garlic, crushed
2 cans cream of mushroom soup
2 cans green chilies, chopped
1 Tbsp. flour
1 large onion, chopped and divided
into halves
1½ cups fresh mushrooms, sliced

2 tsps. salt
2 lbs. small curd cottage cheese
1 cup ripe olives, chopped
4 cups chicken, cooked and in
pieces
1 pkg. flour tortillas (20 to a pkg.)
2 cartons sour cream
8 ozs. Cheddar cheese, grated

Put spinach and broth in a blender, mix several seconds until chopped. In a saucepan, combine spinach mixture with next 4 ingredients, half the onion, a teaspoon of salt, and half a cup of mushrooms; bring this mixture to a boil, stirring constantly, and then, turn burner off. Combine cottage cheese, remaining onions, salt, mushrooms, olives, and chicken; add a cup of spinach mixture, and mix. Grease 3 7x11-inch pyrex dishes. Fill each tortilla with 2 tablespoons of cottage cheese filling, roll tortillas up, and place side by side in the dishes, and cover with remaining spinach sauce. Cook at 350° for approximately 20 minutes or until bubbly. Spread grated cheese on top; put tortillas in oven until cheese melts. Spread sour cream on top, and return to oven for 5 minutes more. Absolutely Wonderful!!
Serves 10-12 generously.

SOUTHERN FRIED CHICKEN

1 2½ lb. fryer, cut up
Buttermilk, enough to cover
  chicken
1 cup flour
1 tsp. salt

¼ tsp. pepper
¼ tsp. paprika
Shortening, 2 inches deep in heavy
  skillet

Soak chicken in buttermilk for 15 to 20 minutes. Heat shortening over medium heat. Combine flour, salt, pepper, and paprika. Roll chicken in flour mixture; place in hot oil, and brown, covered, on one side. Then, turn, and replace cover. Cook chicken over medium heat until tender and brown. Delicious and easy!

CREAM GRAVY

In heavy skillet, put 2-3 tablespoons grease. Over low heat, add 2 tablespoons flour and salt and pepper (to taste). Stir continually, while allowing flour/grease mixture to brown. When brown, add 1 cup of milk; let mixture come to a boil, stirring until desired thickness is reached. If gravy is too thick, add more milk.

"When making gravy, remember that the amount of grease you use depends on how much gravy you need. You can adjust ingredients, proportionately, according to how much grease you use. This cream gravy is delicious, particularly with chicken and over biscuits!!"

Martha Ann McLaurin, Jackson, Mississippi

DOVES WONDERFUL

Doves, 3 per person
Burgundy, enough, when mixed
  with water to cover doves
Water
Onions, chopped, 1 onion per 9-10
  doves

Bacon, ½ slice for each dove
Butter
Salt and pepper

Marinate doves for 10 to 12 hours in a mixture of equal parts of burgundy and water and the onions. The marinade must cover the doves! At the end of marinating, remove doves, saving marinade. Wrap each dove with half slices of bacon, securing with a toothpick. Place doves, breast side down, on a cookie sheet that has been lined with foil. Cook over grate on a covered grill, sprinkling frequently with marinade. Cook until done (about 2 hours). About 15 minutes before doves are done, pour 1 cup of burgundy over them. Truly a Mississippi treat!!

Buddy Morris, Jackson, Mississippi

MISSISSIPPI FACT:
During the Civil War, Mississippi's state government functioned quite well. However, due to the war, the state capital was moved from Jackson to Enterprise to Meridian to Jackson to Meridian to Columbus to Macon to Jackson!!

DUCK JAMBALAYA

3 ducks, boiled, boned, and cut into
   pieces
Salt, black pepper, and cayenne
   pepper, enough to coat ducks
1 cup cooking oil
6 onions, chopped

1 Tbsp. bell pepper, chopped
1 Tbsp. celery
½ lb. (8 ozs.) smoked sausage
3 cups long grain rice, uncooked
4 cups water
Garlic salt

Season ducks with salt and peppers. Heat oil in a heavy skillet until hot; fry duck pieces until brown, keeping burner heat high. Lower heat, and add onion, bell pepper, and celery, cooking until tender. Add sausage, then the rice, and a pinch of salt and pepper. Cook slowly over low heat for 15 minutes, stirring often. Add water, rice, and garlic salt; stir, and cover. Don't stir again! Simmer over low heat for an hour, or until rice is done. Keep covered when serving.
Serves 8.

Buddy Crosby, Jackson, Mississippi

REAL MISSISSIPPI FOLK'S FACT:
Real Mississippi folk never say "Mississippi." They say "Mis-sipi!"

QUAIL AND CREAM

12 quail
6 Tbsps. butter
1 apple, chopped
2 small onions, chopped
¾ cup celery
¼ cup brandy
1 beef bouillon cube

3 Tbsps. flour
1 can chicken broth (Swanson's)
½ tsp. sage
½ tsp. garlic salt
¼ cup vermouth
½-¾ cup cream

Saute quail, vegetables, and apple in butter. Heat brandy, and add to quail and vegetables. Ignite; then, boil down. Next, add flour, then bouillon cube, broth, sage, vermouth, and garlic salt; cook until tender. When done (all tender), add the cream to the gravy. DELICIOUS!

Carolyn McIntyre, Jackson, Mississippi

MISSISSIPPI FACT:
The University of Mississippi ranks second in the South in the number of Rhodes Scholars it has produced.

VENISON CUTLETS

Venison
1 egg (more, if needed)
¼ cup milk (more, if needed)
1 sleeve of a box of saltine
  crackers

Flour
Juice of several lemons
Peanut oil

Slice venison about ¼ inch thick per slice; remove all fat and fascia (white) from the meat. Beat well with a meat tenderizer hammer. Mix egg and an equal amount of milk in a bowl. Crush crackers, and add 1/3 that amount of flour. Dip venison in egg-milk wash, roll in cracker-flour mix, and cook in hot peanut oil in a heavy skillet. When edges are brown, turn venison, and cook until brown. Remove; place on a paper towel to drain. When drained, squeeze lemon juice on cutlets, and serve immediately. OUTSTANDING!

"The biggest problem with this recipe is getting the cooked venison to the table for everyone likes to eat them as soon as the lemon juice goes on!!"

Dr. Heber Simmons, Jr., Jackson, Mississippi

Dr. Simmons is currently President of the American Academy of Pediatric Dentistry. He is an avid hunter and fisherman and is most proud that he has a Grand Slam of North American Sheep!

SENSATIONAL BREAKFAST CASSEROLE

4-6 slices thick whole wheat bread
1 lb. bulk hot sausage (can also use
   bacon or ham)
1 cup sharp Cheddar cheese,
   grated
6 eggs

2 cups milk
1 tsp. salt
Dash of pepper
Dash of cayenne pepper
1 tsp. dry mustard
Paprika

Tear up bread, and place in a 13x9x2-inch pyrex dish. Brown sausage; drain well. Mash up sausage, and spoon over bread; sprinkle with cheese. Beat together eggs, milk, and seasonings, and pour over sausage/cheese mixture. Let sit overnight in the refrigerator. Bake at 350° for 35 to 40 minutes. A great way to start a holiday, weekend, or any day!!
Serves 6.

Judy Greene, Jackson, Mississippi

MISSISSIPPI FESTIVALS:
Trees of Christmas, held in Meridian in the lovely Merrehope (home built in 1867) in December, features an exhibition of the Trees of Christmas displayed throughout.

Christmas at the Old Capitol, held in Jackson in December, features festive live entertainment in the decorated Old Capitol.

WONDERFUL HAM AND CHEESE SOUFFLE

16 slices bread, no crust and cubed
1 lb. ham, cubed
1 lb. sharp Cheddar cheese, grated
1½ cups Swiss cheese, cut in small pieces
6 eggs
3 cups milk
½ tsp. onion salt
½ tsp. dry mustard
3 cups corn flakes, crushed
½ cup butter, melted

Grease a 9x13-inch baking pan. Spread half the bread cubes evenly in the dish. Add ham and both cheeses; cover with remaining bread cubes. Mix eggs, milk, onion salt, and mustard; pour evenly over bread cubes, and refrigerate overnight. Before baking, combine corn flakes and butter. Pour mixture over refrigerated souffle, and bake at 375° for 40 minutes. A super meal with a salad and Pan Rolls (recipe, page 50). DELICIOUS!

Mary Coleman, Jackson, Mississippi

PLANTATION BARBECUE SAUCE

1 (6 oz.) can tomato paste
1 cup water
¼ cup oil
½ cup A-1 Steak Sauce
Juice of 2 lemons
Garlic powder to taste
½ tsp. hot pepper sauce

In a saucepan, combine all ingredients, and simmer for 15 minutes. OUTSTANDING ON CHICKEN , BEEF, AND RIBS!
Yields 2½ cups.

MARY ANN MOBLEY'S BARBECUED SHORT RIBS

3 lbs. short ribs
2 Tbsps. Crisco
¼ cup vinegar
2 Tbsps. brown sugar
1 cup ketchup

½ cup water
3 Tbsps. Worcestershire sauce
1 tsp. mustard
1 cup celery, diced
2 tsps. salt

In a large pan, melt the Crisco; brown ribs. Add remaining ingredients. Cover, and bake for 2 hours at 350⁰ (or at 250⁰ in an electric frying pan). DELICIOUS AND EASY!!

Mary Ann Mobley Collins

Mary Ann Mobley was Miss Mississippi in 1958 and became Miss America of 1959. She was Mississippi's first Miss America!

MISSISSIPPI FACT:
Mississippi has had four talented and lovely young women bear the title of Miss America. Besides Mary Ann Mobley, they are Lynda Lee Mead (1960), Cheryl Prewitt (1980), and Susan Diane Akin (1985).

BLACKENED CATFISH

6 catfish fillets
2 sticks unsalted butter, melted
2 Tbsps. paprika
2½ tsps. salt
1 tsp. onion powder

1½ tsps. garlic powder
1½ tsps. cayenne pepper
2 tsps. lemon pepper
1 tsp. ground thyme
1½ tsps. basil

Heat a large cast iron skillet over high heat until drop of water sizzles in skillet, about 10 minutes. Combine all seasonings. Dip each fillet in butter until both sides are well coated. Using a tablespoon of seasoning per fillet, sprinkle mix on both sides, patting on by hand. Place fillets on waxed paper while preparing others. Place 3 fillets in hot skillet, drizzling each with a tablespoon of butter. There will be a lot of smoke; thus, kitchen should be well ventilated. Cook for about 2 minutes per side; remove cooked fillets to a warm platter, and repeat cooking process with remaining fillets. A wonderful way to prepare Mississippi Farm-Raised Catfish!! *Serves 6.*

Compliments of the Mississippi Catfish Industries
(as appeared in the) CLARION LEDGER-JACKSON DAILY NEWS

MISSISSIPPI FACT AND FESTIVAL:
Belzoni, Mississippi, is the "Catfish Capital of the World." Each year in April, Belzoni holds the World Catfish Festival!

CATFISH SESAME

Catfish fillets (4-5 ozs. per   *Milk*
  serving), fresh or thawed   *Cracker crumbs*
All-purpose flour   *Sesame seeds*
Egg (1 egg per 4-5 fillets)   *Cooking oil or margarine*

Rinse catfish; coat lightly with flour. Combine egg and milk. Separately, combine cracker crumbs and sesame seeds. Dip fish into egg mixture, and roll in crumb mixture. Place dipped and rolled fillets in a single layer in hot oil in a large, shallow baking pan. Bake at 400° for 15 to 20 minutes, or pan fry in oil at 360° for 4 to 5 minutes on each side. GREAT!

Catfish Farmers of America, Jackson, Mississippi

BAKED DIXIELAND CATFISH

6 Farm-Raised Catfish   *12 lemon slices, thinly sliced*
½ cup (Kraft) French Salad Dressing *Paprika*

Brush each catfish inside and out with dressing. Cut 6 lemon slices in half, and place 2 halves in each body cavity. Place fish in a well greased 14x9x2-inch pan, and top each fillet with a slice of lemon. Then, brush each fillet with remaining dressing; sprinkle with paprika. Bake at 350° for 30 to 35 minutes or until catfish flakes easily when tested with a fork. If desired, you may baste with more dressing once or twice while baking. *Serves 6.*

Catfish Farmers of Mississippi, Jackson, Mississippi

BILLY JOE'S FISH CASSEROLE

Fish fillets
1 bottle Seven Seas Creamy
  Caesar Dressing

¼ lb. of grated mild Cheddar
  cheese for each fillet
Crushed potato chips for topping

In a shallow 9x13-inch pyrex dish, place a suitable number of fish fillets (enough to cover the bottom of the dish). Pour salad dressing over fish, coating both sides with the dressing. Cover each fillet with cheese, and top (thoroughly) with potato chips. Heat in a 350⁰ oven for 12 to 15 minutes, and serve. Delicious!!

Dr. Heber Simmons, Jr., Jackson, Mississippi

This fish casserole comes from the collection of Billy Joe Cross, a famous Mississippi cook. Mr. Cross, a former Director of the Mississippi Game and Fish Commission, has published his own recipes in COOKING WILD GAME: MISSISSIPPI STYLE, a delightful collection of fine recipes!!

MISSISSIPPI FACT:
The Farm-Raised Catfish Industry is the fastest growing industry in Mississippi, and Mississippi processes over 90% of the farm-raised catfish produced in the United States!!

HEBER'S RECIPES FOR BEST FRIED FISH

Recipe # 1

Fish fillets
Louisiana Hot Sauce
Nabisco Cracker Meal

Peanut oil
Juice of several lemons

Place fillets in a large pyrex dish; coat liberally with hot sauce, and allow sauce to remain on fish for 10 minutes. Place cracker meal in a ziplock bag, put fillets in the bag, and shake to coat with the crumbs. Fry fillets in HOT peanut oil until they are brown. Drain on paper towels; squeeze lemon juice on fillets immediately!

Recipe # 2

Fish fillets
Buttermilk (for dipping)
Flour (for dipping)

Peanut oil
Juice of several lemons

Dip fillets in buttermilk, and then, in the flour. Repeat process; then, fry fillets in hot oil until they are brown. Squeeze lemon juice on fish, and serve.

Dr. Heber Simmons, Jr., Jackson, Mississippi

MISSISSIPPI FACT:
Unlike other fish, Mississippi Farm-Raised Catfish are scientifically bred for optimum size, flavor, and texture!

SHRIMP AND ARTICHOKE CASSEROLE

2 Tbsps. butter
1 cup heavy cream
¼ tsp. cayenne pepper
Salt to taste
½ tsp. paprika
3 Tbsps. flour
1 Tbsp. catsup

1 cup New York sharp cheese,
 grated
3 Tbsps. sherry
1 Tbsp. lemon juice
1 Tbsp. Lea & Perrins sauce
2-3 lbs. shrimp, cooked and shelled
2 large cans sliced artichoke hearts

Make a sauce by combining first 6 ingredients; cook over low heat, stirring constantly until sauce thickens. Then, add next 5 ingredients, and blend well. Alternate shrimp and artichoke hearts in a greased 2-quart casserole. Cover with cream sauce, and heat in a 350° oven until casserole is bubbly. A great way to treat family and friends to shrimp!
Sereves 6-8.

Dorothy Power Johnson, Hattiesburg, Mississippi

MISSISSIPPI FESTIVAL:
Gumbo Festival of the Universe, held in Necaise Crossing (north of Bay St. Louis) in October, features country and western music, craft booths, a tobacco spitting contest, and a gumbo cooking and eating contest that climaxes with the crowning of the Gumbo Queen and "Little Miss Gumbo!"

MRS. DUGGAN'S CRAB MEAT AU GRATIN

1 stalk celery, chopped
½ cup white onion, chopped
¼ lb. butter
½ cup flour
16 ozs. whipping cream
2 egg yolks

1 tsp. salt
¼ tsp. black pepper
½ tsp. red pepper
1 lb. lump crab meat
½ cup scallions, chopped
½ lb. Cheddar cheese, grated

Saute onions and celery in butter until wilted. Blend in flour, then cream, stirring constantly; add next 6 ingredients. Pour into greased 1-quart casserole; sprinkle with cheese. Bake at 375° for 10 to 15 minutes or until golden brown. *Serves 4-6.*

MR. DUGGAN'S BOILED SHRIMP

5 lbs. shrimp, uncooked, with heads on
3 qts. water (enough to cover shrimp)
1 cup salt
2 boxes crab boil

2 medium onions, sliced
2 lemons, sliced
1 Tbsp. cooking oil
2 Tbsps. cayenne pepper

In a large, heavy pot combine all ingredients, excluding shrimp; bring seasonings to rolling boil, cover, and boil 10 minutes. Add shrimp, and return to a boil. Remove from heat, let stand for 2 minutes; then, drain, remove heads, and serve. The secret to outstanding flavor is to always boil shrimp with the heads on!

Laura and Earl Duggan, Baton Rouge, Louisiana

Mr. Duggan comes to Jackson almost every weekend and sells fresh seafood from his truck. There is a scramble for his fresh seafood, and he always leaves Jackson with an empty truck!!

FAVORITE SEAFOOD LAGNIAPPE

1 lb. spaghittini (thin pasta)
½ cup butter
½ cup flour
1 cup chicken broth
1 cup heavy cream
1 cup Swiss cheese, shredded
4 Tbsps. sherry

Salt and pepper
1 large can mushrooms
3 Tbsps. butter
3 lbs. shrimp, peeled and cleaned
1½ lbs. crab meat
8 ozs. Parmesan cheese, shredded
Slivered almonds

Cook spaghittini; drain. Make a cream sauce by combining butter, flour, broth, and cream. Cook mixture over low heat, stirring until sauce thickens. Blend in Swiss cheese, sherry, salt and pepper to taste; add mushrooms, and set aside. Saute shrimp and crab meat in 3 tablespoons butter until shrimp are cooked (10 minutes or so). Add seafood to cream mixture, and pour into a large, buttered casserole; sprinkle with almonds and Parmesan cheese. Bake at 350° until bubbly; serve hot. The recipe can be halved.

Serves 6-8 amply!   Gertrude Wiggins, Pascagoula, Mississippi

MISSISSIPPI FACT:
Mississippi's largest company in terms of employment and revenue is the Ingalls Shipbuilding Corporation of Pascagoula. Ingalls was the first company to build all-welded ships for the United States Navy and was the first company in the South to build a nuclear submarine!!

DESSERTS

BUTTERMILK POUND CAKE

1 cup butter
3 cups sugar
5 egg yolks, well beaten
1 cup buttermilk
3 cups flour

5 egg whites, well beaten
1/3 tsp. soda (dissolved in buttermilk)
2 tsps. vanilla
Powdered sugar, optional

Cream butter and sugar; then, add egg yolks. Add flour and milk alternately. Next, blend in egg whites and vanilla. Pour into a greased Bundt pan that has been dusted with powdered sugar. Cook in a 325° oven for an hour and 10 minutes or until a fork, inserted into cake, comes out clean. Cool; then, sprinkle top of cake with powdered sugar. WONDERFUL!! Cake is great sliced and toasted at breakfast!

Katherine Travis, McComb, Mississippi

FUDGE CAKE

1½ cups butter, softened
6 eggs
1½ cups sugar
2 cups flour, sifted

3 1/3 cups chocolate fudge frosting mix (or 2½ pkgs.)
2 cups pecans, chopped

In a large bowl, cream butter, adding eggs one at a time, beating well after each addition. Gradually add sugar, beating at high speed until mixture is light and fluffy. By hand, stir in flour, dry frosting mix, and nuts until all are well blended. Bake in a greased, 12 cup Bundt pan at 350° for 60 to 65 minutes. Cake is done when it has a dry, shiny brownie-type crust.

Dottie Cates, Jackson, Mississippi

COCA—COLA CAKE

1 *Duncan Hines Swiss Chocolate Cake Mix*	½ *cup Crisco oil*
	1¼ *cups water*
1 *pkg. instant vanilla mix*	2 *eggs*

Preheat oven to 350°. Spray a 13x9-inch oblong pan with Pam. Blend all ingredients in a large bowl; beat at medium speed until batter is well mixed. Bake for about an hour or until a fork, inserted, comes out clean. Frost with Coca Cola Icing.

COCA-COLA ICING

6 *Tbsps. Coca Cola*	2 *Tbsps. cocoa*
1 *stick margarine*	1 *cup nuts, chopped*
1(16 oz.) *box Confectioner's sugar*	

Heat coke and margarine until they boil. Sift cocoa and sugar together; pour coke mixture over sugar mixture, and blend well. Add nuts. Cover top of cake with frosting, and serve from pan.

Nellah Taylor, Starkville, Mississippi

MISSISSIPPI FACTS:

In 1894, the first Coca-Cola was bottled at the Biedenharn Candy Company in Vicksburg!

Root beer was invented in Biloxi by Edward A. Barq, Sr., in 1898!

FIVE FLAVOR POUND CAKE

2 sticks margarine
½ cup Crisco (solid)
3 cups sugar
3 cups flour (plain, not self-rising)
1 cup milk
5 large eggs, well beaten

½ tsp. baking powder
1 Tbsp. vanilla extract
1 Tbsp. butter flavoring
1 Tbsp. coconut extract
1 Tbsp. lemon flavoring
1 Tbsp. rum flavoring

Have all ingredients at room temperature, and preheat oven to 325°. Cream margarine, shortening, and sugar; add eggs. Sift flour and baking powder. Alternately, add flour mixture and milk to creamed mixture, ending with dry ingredients. Blend in extracts and flavorings. Grease a tube pan well with solid shortening and flour; line bottom of pan with brown paper. Bake for 1½ hours. Cool for an hour. Punch holes in top for icing.

FIVE FLAVOR ICING

1 cup sugar
½ cup water
½ tsp. vanilla extract
½ tsp. butter flavoring

½ tsp. coconut extract
½ tsp. lemon flavoring
½ tsp. rum flavoring

Combine all ingredients. Bring to a boil; boil for 2 minutes (be sure to time), stirring constantly. Drizzle over top and sides of cake. Outstanding!!

Dotte Cates, Jackson, Mississippi

GERMAN CHOCOLATE CAKE WITH CHOCOLATE PECAN ICING

1 box Betty Crocker's German   *1 tsp. almond flavoring*
Chocolate Cake Mix

Make cake according to package's directions, adding almond flavoring to batter. Pour into a greased, floured 12-cup Bundt cake pan. Bake 43 minutes in a preheated 350⁰ oven. Then, remove from oven, and cool for 10 minutes before icing.

CHOCOLATE PECAN ICING

½ cup butter   *1 tsp. vanilla extract*
¼ cup plus 2 Tbsps. milk   *1 tsp. almond flavoring*
¼ cup cocoa   *¾ cup pecans, chopped*
¾ (16 oz.) pkg. powdered sugar,
sifted

Combine butter, milk, and cocoa in a heavy saucepan, over medium heat, and bring to a good boil. Remove from heat, stir in powdered sugar, extract, flavoring and pecans. Spread over warm cake.
Serves 20.

From the Kitchen of Winifred Green Cheney, Jackson, Mississippi

MISSISSIPPI FACT:
Winifred Green Cheney is one of Mississippi's most treasured cooks. Her two cookbooks, THE SOUTHERN HOSPITALITY COOKBOOK and COOKING FOR COMPANY, published by SOUTHERN LIVING MAGAZINE, are outstanding. Mrs. Cheney is also featured in A COOK'S TOUR OF MISSISSIPPI.

HERSHEY BAR CAKE

6 plain Hershey Bars
1 (16 oz.) Hershey Chocolate
   Syrup
2 cups sugar
2 sticks margarine
4 eggs

2½ cups flour
½ tsp. baking soda
¼ tsp. salt
1 cup buttermilk
2 tsps. vanilla
Cocoa (optional)

In the top of a double boiler, melt Hershey Bars in syrup; cool. Cream sugar and margarine well; add eggs, folding in one at a time. Mix flour with salt and soda; sift. Add flour mixture, alternating with buttermilk, to creamed mixture. Pour into a greased and dusted (I always dust with cocoa.) Bundt or tube pan. Bake at 350° for an hour and 15 minutes. Let cake cool in pan. This pretty cake is excellent served with vanilla ice cream!

From the recipes of Eddieth Davis, Pascagoula, Mississippi

MISSISSIPPI FACT:

The Deep Sea Fishing Rodeo, in Gulfport, in July, is one the largest fishing contests in the South.

MISSISSIPPI APPLE CAKE

2 eggs
2 cups sugar
1 stick butter or margarine
3 cups raw apples, chopped into
small pieces

2½ cups flour, sifted
1 cup sour milk
3 tsps. cinnamon
1½ tsps. soda

Cream sugar and butter; add eggs, one at a time, and continue beating. Add soda and cinnamon to flour. Alternate flour and milk as (you) add to creamed mixture; then, add apples. Grease the bottom of a 12x9x2-inch pan; cover with waxed paper. Pour in the batter, and cook at 325° for 50 to 60 minutes. Cover with Best Topping.

BEST TOPPING

1 cup coconut
2/3 cup brown sugar
½ cup cream or canned milk

3 Tbsps. margarine or butter
½ tsp. vanilla

Cream sugar and butter; add cream and vanilla. Lastly add coconut. Spread topping over cake, and put cake back in oven long enough for sugar to melt.

"This is a delicious cake. When warmed, it can be served with cream or hot rum sauce. It's even better the second day!!"

Ann Rushing, Mississippi Department of Agriculture and Commerce

RED VELVET CAKE

½ tsp. butter
1½ cups sugar
1 tsp. vanilla extract
2 eggs
1 (3 oz.) bottle red food coloring
2 heaping tsps. cocoa

2½ cups cake flour
1 tsp. salt
1 cup buttermilk
1 tsp. soda
1 Tbsp. vinegar

Cream butter, sugar, and vanilla; add eggs one at a time, and mix well. Make a thin paste with cocoa and food coloring, and add to creamed mixture. Sift flour and salt together; add flour mixture and buttermilk, one tablespoon at a time, to creamed mixture beginning and ending with flour. Mix soda and vinegar; blend into cake mixture. Grease and flour waxed paper that will line 2 8-inch pans. Bake at 350° for 20 to 30 minutes. Cool.

ICING

4½ Tbsps. flour
1½ cups milk

1½ cups sugar
1½ cups butter

1½ tsps. vanilla extract

Make a thick paste with flour mixed with a small amount of milk. Gradually, add remaining milk. Cook in the top of a double boiler, beating until thick. Set aside to cool. Cream butter, sugar, and vanilla, beating until fluffy. Add cooled mixture, and continue beating until consistency is like whipped cream. Cool before icing cake.

Sherye Simmons Green
MISS MISSISSIPPI, 1979

WHITE CAKE WITH COCONUT ICING

1 Duncan Hines White Cake Mix
2 eggs
1 (14 oz.) can Eagle Brand
condensed milk

1 (12 oz.) carton Cool Whip
1 (14 oz.) bag coconut

Make cake according to package's directions, adding eggs. Bake in a 9x13-inch pyrex pan. While cake is hot, poke holes in it with a fork. Then, pour condensed milk over cake. Let cake cool; then, frost by covering with Cool Whip. Sprinkle with coconut. This cake can be made in a Bundt pan and looks very elegant! It is wonderful and easy!!

Mary Hopton, Jackson, Mississippi

SCRUMPTIOUS, GOOEY BUTTER CAKE

1 box yellow cake mix
1 egg, slightly beaten
1 stick butter, melted
1 (8 oz.) pkg. cream cheese

1 box (3½ cups) powdered sugar,
reserving 2 Tbsps. for top of cake
2 eggs

Mix cake mix, egg, and butter together until crumbly. Then press into a greased 9x13-inch pan. Mix cream cheese, sugar, and 2 eggs together; pour over cake dough in the pan. Bake at 350⁰ for 30 to 40 minutes. After cake cools, sprinkle top with reserved powdered sugar.

"This cake takes 10 minutes to prepare, and people, after having a slice, think that you spent hours making it!"

Lacey Morris, GREAT FLAVORS OF MISSISSIPPI

DELECTABLE MINI CHEESE CAKES

16 ozs. cream cheese
24 vanilla wafers
¾ cup sugar
2 eggs

1 tsp. vanilla
1 (16 oz.) can cherry pie filling
24 muffin baking cups

Put a vanilla wafer in each muffin cup. Mix cream cheese, sugar, eggs, and vanilla with an electric mixer; put a tablespoon of mixture on each wafer. Top with pie filling. Bake at 375° for 15 minutes. Let cool before removing cheese cakes from muffin cups. You may substitute your favorite pie filling for the topping. Makes 24 delightful little cheese cakes!

Pat Quinn, Jackson, Mississippi

HALLELUJAH PIE

1 can Comstock Apple Pie Filling
1 can blueberry pie filling
1 ½ sticks margarine

1 box cake mix (yellow or white)
1 cup pecans, chopped
2 tsps. cinnamon

Pour both cans of filling into a long (13½x8¾-inch) pan. Pour dry cake mix over fillings, sprinkling cinnamon over mixture and blending slightly. Sprinkle pecans on top, and place pats of margarine over entire top of mixture. Bake at 350° for 30 to 40 minutes or until golden brown. Serve hot or cold (I prefer cold!).Top with ice cream. When making Hallelujah Pie, you may substitute other pie fillings. MARVELOUS AND EASY!
Serves 6-8.

Gertrude Wiggins, Pascagoula, Mississippi

MOCHA ICE CREAM DESSERT

24 oreo cookies, crushed
½ gallon coffee ice cream, softened
1/3 cup butter, melted
3 ozs. unsweetened chocolate
2 Tbsps. butter
1 cup sugar
Dash of salt

2 (5½-6 oz.) cans evaporated milk
2 tsps. vanilla
1½ cups heavy cream, whipped
1½ ozs. kahlua
Powdered sugar to taste
½-¾ nuts, chopped

Combine cookie crumbs and butter; press into the bottom of a buttered 9x13-inch pan. Refrigerate until chilled; spoon in ice cream, and freeze. Melt butter and chocolate; add sugar, salt, and milk. Bring to boil, stirring until thickened. Remove mixture from heat, and add vanilla. Chill mixture; spread over ice cream. Freeze. Add kahlua and sugar to whipped cream; spread over chocolate layer, sprinkle top with nuts, and freeze.

Kittye Wright, Columbus, Mississippi

GRAPE SHERBET

1½ cups grape juice concentrate
9 ozs. Cool Whip

½ gallon pineapple sherbet

Soften sherbet; then, combine all ingredients in a large mixing bowl. Mix well with an electric mixer on low speed. Pour mixture into plastic cartons, and freeze.
Serves 6-8.

Mildred Gould Creekmore, Jackson, Mississippi

AIMEE'S GREEN CREAM

4 eggs, extra large
1 1/3 cups sugar
2 qts. whole milk
½ pt. cream
1 Tbsp. vanilla extract

1 Tbsp. almond extract
Green food coloring (Amount you
   use depends on how dark you
   want ice cream; 1 capful to start.)

Beat eggs until light. Add sugar, beat again, and then, add a quart of milk. Cook over boiling water until mixture coats a spoon. Cool; then, add remaining milk and the cream. Add extracts and food coloring. Freeze in either a hand crank or electric ice cream freezer. Everyone loves this!!

Margaret Lowery, Jackson, Mississippi

PEACH ICE CREAM

1 qt. cream, whipped
2½ cups sugar, divided equally

3 peaches, finely chopped
Pinch of salt

Scald whipping cream in top of double boiler. Then, add 1¼ cups of sugar; mix well. Pour cream mixture into a gallon freezer; freeze until thickened. Puree peaches in a blender; add rest of sugar and pinch of salt, stirring until sugar is dissolved. Stir peaches mixture into cream mixture. Cover; freeze until firm. This ice cream is worth the effort!!

Siclily Morris, Jackson, Mississippi

ESSIE'S ICE CREAM

8 large eggs
2½ cups sugar
½ gallon milk

1 pt. whipping cream
2 tsps. vanilla extract

Mix eggs, sugar, and milk until smooth and very well blended. Cook mixture in the top of a double boiler until it thickens. DO NOT BE ALARMED if mixture curdles for this will not bother taste and will smooth when frozen. Add whipping cream and vanilla before placing mixture in ice cream freezer. So Good!

Dr. Heber Simmons, Jr., Jackson, Mississippi

A Tip From Dr. Simmons:
When preparing homemade ice cream, place finished ice cream in small or large styrofoam cups. Cover with a small square of aluminum foil, and place in freezer. Before serving, take from freezer, and remove the foil. Place the cup of ice cream in microwave on a high setting for 30 seconds. The ice cream will then have consistency of freshly frozen cream.

MISSISSIPPI FESTIVAL:

OKTOC Country Store, in Starkville in November, is an old fashioned bazaar with handcrafted items, home baked goods, and Brunswick Stew for everyone!

WINIFRED GREEN CHENEY'S CREAMY BAKED CUSTARD WITH MERINGUE

8 rounded tsps. firmly packed,
dark brown sugar
3 large egg yolks and 1 whole egg
or 4 large eggs

½ cup sugar
3 cups whole milk
1½ tsps. vanilla extract
Ground nutmeg

Place teaspoon of brown sugar in each custard cup. Break eggs into large bowl, add sugar, and beat lightly with a wire whisk. Add remaining ingredients except for nutmeg; beat lightly until well blended. Ladle into cups; sprinkle with nutmeg. Place cups in enough hot water to come halfway up the outside of each cup; bake in a preheated 300⁰ oven for 30 to 35 minutes or until a knife inserted 1 inch from edge of cup comes out clean. Serve hot or cold. Yields 8 (6 oz.) custard "cups full."

MERINGUE

2 egg whites, room temperature
⅛ tsp. salt

¼ tsp. cream of tartar
¼ cup sugar

Beat egg whites, salt, and tartar with an electric mixer at high speed until whites stand in soft peaks. Add sugar gradually, continue beating until whites are stiff but not dry. Spread lightly over custard in cups. Do not spread meringue to edge of cup; bake in preheated 325⁰ oven for 10 minutes; allow custard and meringue to cool on wire rack; chill in refrigerator. For a fancy custard, omit nutmeg, and top with a teaspoon of orange marmalade or a favorite preserve, and cover with meringue.

TRUDY'S FANTASTIC BREAD PUDDING

10 slices white bread, torn into
    pieces
1¼ cups sugar
4 eggs, beaten until fluffy
1/3 cup margarine, melted
2 Tbsps. coconut

¼ cup raisins, soaked overnight in
    2 Tbsps. light rum
1 (13 oz.) can Carnation
    Evaporated Milk
2 tsps. vanilla extract
2 cups milk

Soak bread and coconut in both milks. To eggs, add sugar; beat until slightly thickened. Add vanilla and margarine. Mix well; stir into bread/milk mixture. Stir well; add raisins. Let whole mixture sit for 5 minutes; pour into 2-quart casserole, and bake at 425° for 25 minutes.

Trudy Wiggins Pascale, Native of Pascagoula, Mississippi

FUDGE PUDDING

4 eggs
2 cups sugar
½ cup flour
1 cup pecans, chopped

¾ cup butter
2 heaping Tbsps. cocoa
1 tsp. vanilla
Dash of salt

In a mixing bowl, combine first 4 ingredients. In a saucepan, melt remaining ingredients. Combine both mixtures, and pour into an ungreased 9x13-inch pan. Put pan into another pan that has water in it; bake at 350° for an hour and 10 minutes. Serve upside down.
Serves 6-8.

Meredith Creekmore, Jackson, Mississippi

WHITE CHOCOLATE MOUSSE

1½ cups sugar
¾ cup water
Pinch of cream of tartar
18 ozs. white chocolate, finely
    chopped

7 egg whites
1 qt. whipped cream
5 ozs. Grand Marnier

Combine sugar, water, and tartar in a small saucepan, and bring mixture to 230°. Just before temperature reaches 230°, begin whipping egg whites into stiff peaks. Slowly drizzle sugar mixture into egg whites while beating them. Begin adding white chocolate to egg whites, and fold in by hand. Then, place mixture in freezer. Combine whipped cream with Grand Marnier; fold mixture into white chocolate mixture. Return to freezer for at least an hour before serving.

RASPBERRY SAUCE

24 ozs. fresh raspberries (You may
    use frozen.)

1/3 cup corn starch, mixed with a
    little warm water

In a saucepan, bring raspberries to a boil. Remove from heat, and strain through a China cap or any fine mesh strainer. Again, bring berries to a boil adding corn starch. Remove from burner; cool. Serve with mousse, and remember to reserve some fresh raspberries for garnishing.

Nick's Restaurant, Jackson, Mississippi

SUGARED PECANS

3 cups sugar
1 cup water
1/3 cup orange juice

1 tsp. orange rind
1 lb. pecans, sliced

Mix sugar, water, and juice; boil to soft ball stage or 240° on a candy thermometer. Remove from burner, add orange rind and pecans, and stir until syrup looks cloudy. Pour onto heavy waxed paper as mixture cools. Break apart. DELICIOUS!

PECAN GLAZE

3 cups sugar
½ tsp. cream of tartar
1 cup water

Pecans, shelled and nut meats in perfect halves

In a saucepan, combine sugar, tartar, and water; stir as mixture heats until sugar dissolves. Wipe away any sugar crystals that may form on the side when dripped from a spoon. Using a long, sharp pin, dip pecan halves, one at a time, into glaze, and place on a buttered dish. Work fast for glaze hardens rapidly! Dates, almonds, Brazil nuts, Malaga grapes, orange sections, and even violets may be treated in this way! This is one of the most delightful ways of using pecans!!

NATCHEZ RECIPES COOKBOOK, Altar Guild, Trinity Episcopal Church
Natchez, Mississippi

MISSISSIPPI FESTIVAL:
The Great River Road Craft Fair, held in Natchez in October, features handmade crafts, furniture, and art for sale by craftsmen from throughout the United States.

MISSISSIPPI MUD FOOL'S FUDGE

¾ cup graham cracker crumbs
1 cup smooth peanut butter
2 sticks margarine, melted

1 box powdered sugar
1 (12 oz.) pkg. semi-sweet
  chocolate chips

Mix well cracker crumbs, peanut butter, and sugar; add margarine, mixing thoroughly. Firmly press mixture into a 9x12-inch pan. Melt chocolate chips in top of a double boiler. Pour melted chocolate over peanut butter. Let cool at room temperature before slicing into squares.

Mary Hopton, Jackson, Mississippi

GREAT FLAVOR'S QUICK CRUNCH CANDY

1 cup sugar
1 cup butter
4 Tbsps. water

1 tsp. vanilla
3 (4 oz.) milk chocolate bars
¾ cup nuts, finely chopped

Put first 4 ingredients in a saucepan. Stir gently over low heat until butter melts and sugar dissolves. Continue to cook until mixture is rather brown or a little, tested in cold water, is very brittle. Pour into a buttered, oblong pan, (We use a 11½x7½x⅞-inch pan.) and while still hot (after about 3 minutes), place chocolate bars on top of mixture. Then, sprinkle with nuts. When candy is cold, break into pieces.

KNOCK YOU NAKEDS

1 pkg. German chocolate cake mix
1 cup nuts, chopped
1/3 cup evaporated milk
¾ cup butter, melted

60 pieces caramel candy
½ cup evaporated milk
1 cup chocolate chips

Combine, and mix well cake mix, nuts, 1/3 cup milk, and butter. Press half of mixture into the bottom of a greased 9x13-inch pyrex dish; bake at 350° for 8 minutes. Melt caramel candy in top of double boiler with half cup of milk. When caramel mixture is well mixed, pour over baked mixture. Cover with chocolate chips, and pour rest of dough on top of chips. Bake for 18 minutes at 350°. Cool before slicing. QUITE SIMPLY DIVINE!
Yields 18-20 squares.

AUNT VI'S BROWNIES

1½ sticks butter, melted
3 squares chocolate, melted
2 cups sugar
Dash of salt
2 eggs, beaten

1 cup flour
2 eggs beaten
1 tsp. vanilla
1 cup nuts

Mix in order listed above. In a 9x9-inch pan, bake brownies at 350° for approximately 40 to 45 minutes, i.e., until the top cracks around the edge. Super good and easy!
Yields 18-20 squares.

Sandy Smith Norton, Jackson, Mississippi

SOPHIE'S BIG COOKIES

2 sticks margarine
4 cups flour
1 cup shortening
1 box light brown sugar
2 cups white sugar
4 eggs

2 tsps. vanilla extract
2 tsps. baking powder
2 cups oatmeal
2 cups corn flakes
1 cup coconut
1 (12 oz.) pkg. chocolate chips

Combine and mix well first 10 ingredients. Then, add remaining ingredients, and blend. Using ¼ cup of mixture per cookie, arrange 6 cookies on a lightly greased cookie sheet. Bake for 15 minutes at 350° until cookies are lightly browned. *Yields about 25-26 giant cookies.*

"These cookies are enormous, fun, and delicious! They make wonderful gifts for birthdays, holidays, really any occasion."

Sophie Sistrunk, Jackson, Mississippi

MISSISSIPPI FACT:

Mississippi is blessed with more than 300,000 acres of rivers, streams, lakes and reservoirs which combined with the white sand beaches of the Gulf Coast provide a wealth of statewide facilities for many different water sports and activities.

COCONUT MACAROONS

3 egg whites
1 cup sugar
1 heaping Tbsp. cornstarch

1¾ cups coconut
1 tsp. vanilla

Beat egg whites until fluffy peaks form, add sugar and cornstarch, and beat all together. Cook in the top of a double boiler for 12 minutes, stirring constantly. Add coconut and vanilla. Drop by spoonfuls onto a buttered cookie sheet. Bake at 300° for 15 minutes. Worth the effort!

Agnes Bowe, Mineral Wells, Mississippi

HOLIDAY FRUIT COOKIES

2 sticks margarine
2 cups brown sugar
2 eggs
½ cup sour milk
3½ cups all-purpose flour

1 tsp. baking soda
½ tsp. salt
1½ cups pecans, chopped
2 cups candied cherries, chopped
2 cups dates, chopped

Mix margarine, sugar, and eggs; add milk. Combine flour, soda, and salt, and stir into margarine mixture. Add pecans, cherries, and dates; blend. Then, chill. On a greased cookie sheet and using a teaspoon, drop the dough 2 inches apart. Preheat oven to 400°, and bake cookies for 8 to 10 minutes. So delicious and pretty!
Yields 7-8 dozen.

Sicily Morris, Jackson, Mississippi

OOEY—GOOEY CHOCOLATE COOKIES

6 Tbsps. butter (no substitutes!)
1 can Eagle Brand condensed milk
1 (12 oz.) pkg. chocolate chips
1 cup flour, rounded

In a saucepan over medium heat, whip together first 3 ingredients. When chocolate is melted and mixture is well blended, remove from burner; add flour. Let mixture "sit" a few minutes. Drop batter, a spoonful at a time, onto an ungreased cookie sheet. Cook at 300° for 6 to 7 minutes or until each cookie is firm, but still gooey. CHOCOLATE LOVERS WILL FIND THESE COOKIES IRRESISTIBLE!!!
Yields approximately 3 dozen cookies.

Ann Toy Morris, Jackson, Mississippi

PEANUT BUTTER-CHIP COOKIES

¾ cup margarine
1 cup sugar
1 cup (packed) light brown sugar
2 eggs
1 Tbsp. vanilla
2 cups flour
1 tsp. baking soda
1 (12 oz.) pkg. peanut butter chips

Cream margarine and sugars together until fluffy. Add eggs and vanilla; beat well. Combine flour and baking soda; then, add to sugars' mixture. Slowly stir in peanut butter chips; drop, a spoonful at a time, onto an ungreased cookie sheet. Bake at 350° for 12 minutes. Remove from cookie sheet when done. So good and different!

Hattie Barnhill, Starkville, Mississippi

GRANDMA TILLOU'S MOLASSES SPICE COOKIES

¾ cup Crisco
1 cup sugar
1 egg, well beaten
¼ cup molasses

2 cups flour
1½ tsps. baking soda
½ tsp. salt
1 tsp. ginger

1 tsp. cloves
1 tsp. cinnamon
Currant jelly

Cream shortening and sugar; add egg and molasses; mix well. Sift dry ingredients together; add to molasses mixture, stirring well. Chill mixture for 2 hours in refrigerator before baking. Make dough into balls about the size of a walnut. Put some sugar into a medium sized paper sack, put 6 to 8 balls into sack, and shake until balls are well coated with sugar. Repeat process until all dough balls are coated with sugar. Put balls on a greased cookie sheet about 2 inches apart; make an indentation in the center of each ball with a small spoon (Be sure not to break dough.), and put a small amount of currant jelly in each indentation. Bake in preheated 350° oven for 8 to 10 minutes. Prepare second sheet of cookies while first is cooking. Cool before removing from cookie sheets.

Yields 4 dozen cookies that can't be beat!

"Some of my happiest childhood memories revolve around my grandmother's making these cookies for me. They are my absolute favorites and are so nice to have during the holidays and to give to friends!!"

Jeanne Verlenden, GREAT FLAVORS OF MISSISSIPPI

BLACK BOTTOM PIE

CRUST:

14 Ginger Snaps   *5 Tbsps. butter, melted*

Crush ginger snaps; roll crumbs out finely. Add butter; pat mixture into 9-inch pie plate.

FIRST MIXTURE:

2 cups milk, scalded   *1½ Tbsps. cornstarch*
4 egg yolks, beaten   *½ square bitter chocolate*
½ cup sugar   *1 tsp. vanilla extract*

Add yolks slowly to hot milk. Combine; stir in sugar and cornstarch. Cook slowly in top of double boiler for 20 minutes, stirring occasionally until mixture coats spoon. Remove custard mixture from heat; measure out 1 cup. Add chocolate to cup of custard mixture; beat mixture well while it cools. Add vanilla; pour into pie crust.

SECOND MIXTURE:

1 Tbsp. gelatin   *2 Tbsps. whiskey*
2 Tbsps. cold water   *1 pint whipping cream,*
4 egg whites   * whipped*
½ cup sugar   *1 oz. bitter chocolate*
¼ tsp. cream of tartar

Dissolve gelatin in water; add remaining custard mixture; cool. Beat egg whites with sugar; add tartar and whiskey; fold into plain custard mixture on top of chocolate mixture; chill. Cover top of pie with whipped cream, and sprinkle with shavings of bitter chocolate. ENJOY!!

Old Southern Tea Room, Vicksburg, Mississippi

DERBY PIE

1 cup sugar
½ cup flour
1 stick butter, melted and cooled
2 eggs, slightly beaten
1 cup chocolate chips

1 cup pecans, chopped
1 tsp. vanilla
1 9-inch pie shell, unbaked
Vanilla ice cream or Cool Whip
(optional)

Combine and stir flour and sugar; add melted butter. Add next 4 ingredients, mixing thoroughly. Pour into pie shell (recipe, page 150). Bake for 50 minutes to an hour at 325⁰. Be careful not to overcook! Wonderful by itself or topped with either ice cream or Cool Whip.

Jane Winston, Jackson, Mississippi

AUNT ERNIE'S FUDGE PIE

½ cup butter
1 square chocolate
1 cup sugar
2 eggs, beaten

1 scant tsp. vanilla extract
½ cup flour
Pecans to taste (optional)
Whipped cream (optional)

Melt butter and chocolate together. Add remaining ingredients; combine well. Pour into a greased 9-inch pyrex pie dish. Cook at 325⁰ for 30 to 40 minutes. When serving, top with whipped cream.

Emmye Bowe Simmons Baker, Native of Cleveland, Mississippi

CHOCOLATE CHESS PIE

1½ cups sugar
1 stick butter
3½ Tbsps. cocoa
1 tsp. vanilla

1 small can
  evaporated milk
2 eggs, beaten

Stir all ingredients together well; pour into an unbaked pie shell. Bake at 325⁰ for 45 minutes. Serve topped with whipped cream. No fail and delicious!

Kittye Wright, Columbus, Mississippi

HERSHEY BAR PIE

6 Hershey Bars with Almonds
½ cup milk
10 large marshmallows

1 (8 oz.) box Nabisco Famous
  Chocolate Wafers
1 (8 oz.) carton Cool Whip

Grind up wafers in blender or food processor; then, firmly mold into pie plate for crust, reserving a few crumbs for the top of the pie. Over a low burner, combine milk with candy bars and marshmallows. Stir often; when candy is completely melted, pour chocolate mixture into chocolate crumb pie crust. Cool; then, top with Cool Whip, and sprinkle with reserved chocolate crumbs. Refrigerate. Absolutely mouth watering!!

Carolyn McIntyre & Lacey Morris, Jackson, Mississippi

OLD FASHIONED PECAN PIE

3 eggs, beaten
1 cup light or dark corn syrup
Pinch of salt
1 cup granulated sugar

1 cup pecan halves
1 tsp. vanilla
9-inch pie shell, unbaked

Preheat oven to 300°. Beat eggs and sugar until thick. Add syrup, salt, and vanilla. Arrange pecans in bottom of pastry shell; add syrup mixture, and bake at 300° until mixture is set, about 50 to 60 minutes. The nuts will rise to top of pie filling, and form a delicious crusted layer!

"This is an old, old way of making pecan pie which you won't find in many cookbooks outside the pecan area!!"

Sternberg Pecan Company, Jackson, Mississippi

MISSISSIPPI FRUIT COBBLER

1 (16 oz.) can of your favorite fruit
   in juice
1½ cups sugar

¾ cup self-rising flour
1 stick margarine
¾ cup sweet milk

Melt margarine in a deep pie dish. Then, mix 1 cup of sugar with milk and flour to make dough. Pour dough over margarine. Pour can of fruit (cherry, peach, apple, blueberry, etc.) on top of dough, and sprinkle with remaining sugar. Bake at 350° until golden brown. SO GOOD AND EASY!

Annie Bess Carnes, Fayette, Mississippi

LEMONADE PIE

1 (6 oz.) can frozen pink lemonade,
    partially thawed
1 can Eagle Brand condensed milk

1 (8 oz.) carton Cool Whip
1 graham cracker crust

Mix lemonade and milk together well. Add Cool Whip. Pour into graham cracker crust, and freeze. You may substitute limeade for lemonade. A great frozen dessert!

Stella Bridges, McComb, Mississippi

JEFFERSON DAVIS PIE

3 eggs, whipped
1 cup sugar
1 heaping Tbsp. flour
1 cup milk, scalded

1 Tbsp. butter
½-1 tsp. vanilla extract or nutmeg
    flavoring

Mix well sugar and flour; add to eggs, beating well. Add butter to scalded milk; combine milk with egg mixture, and blend in vanilla or nutmeg. Bake in an unbaked pie shell (pastry recipe, page 150) for 25 minutes at 325°. Truly Southern and good!

Eschol Stegall, Flora, Mississippi

MISSISSIPPI FACT:
Flora welcomes many visitors each year! They come to view Mississippi's Petrified Forest which surrounds Flora. It's gorgeous!

MINCEMEAT CHEESE PIE

4 (3 oz.) pkgs. cream cheese
2 eggs
½ cup plus 2 Tbsps. sugar
Peel of 1 lemon, grated
1 Tbsp. lemon juice

2 cups mincemeat
1 cup sour cream
½ tsp. vanilla
1 9-inch pie shell, baked (recipe, page 150)

With electric mixer, beat together cheese, eggs, half a cup sugar, lemon peel, and juice. Do not stop until mixture is very smooth. Spoon mincemeat into pie shell, and pour cheese mixture evenly over mincemeat. Bake at 375° for 20 minutes. While mincemeat is cooking, mix together sour cream, 2 tablespoons sugar, and vanilla. When pie has baked, remove from oven, and spread sour cream mixture evenly over the top. Return to oven for 10 minutes. Chill the pie before serving. RICH AND FABULOUS!!
Serves 8 generously.

Elizabeth Steadman Owings, Jackson, Mississippi

MISSISSIPPI FESTIVAL:

Crop Day in Greenwood, Mississippi, in August, remembers when Cotton was King and opens Cotton Row for tours, features demonstrations of the art of cotton classing by hand, arts, crafts, and the opportunity to eat barbecue on Cotton Row!

FLAKY PIE CRUST

3 cups all purpose flour, unsifted
1 cup Crisco shortening
1 tsp. salt
1 tsp. vinegar

1 egg, slightly beaten
1 cup ice water (more if flour
   remains too dry)

Sift flour and salt together. Cut Crisco into flour mixture until mixture looks like corn meal. Add vinegar and water to egg, and mix. Then, add egg mixture gradually to flour mixture; mix all just enough to hold dough together. Separate into 3 or 4 equal sized balls; roll out, and place in pie pans. Pie crusts, not needed, may be frozen in covered pie pans or the balls, wrapped in Saran Wrap. Makes 3 (9-inch) or 4 (8-inch) pie crusts.

Hattie Barnhill, Starkville, Mississippi

TUPELO'S CREAM CHEESE PASTRY

1 stick butter, softened
1 (3 oz.) pkg. Philadelphia Cream
   Cheese, softened

1 cup plus 1 Tbsp. flour

Mix butter and cream cheese together well. Then, add the flour, combining well. This will keep well in the refrigerator.
Yields 1 9-inch pie crust.

From the Recipes of Ernestine Simmons, Tupelo, Mississippi

ORDER CARD

GREAT FLAVORS SERIES OF COOKBOOKS
Post Office Box 922
Pine Bluff, Arkansas 71613

_____ copies of GREAT FLAVORS OF MISSISSIPPI at $9.50 each
_____ copies of GREAT FLAVORS OF LOUISIANA at $9.50 each   _____
_____ copies of GREAT FLAVORS OF TEXAS at $10.50 each   _____
                                                      TOTAL   _____

EACH PER COPY PRICE INCLUDES POSTAGE, HANDLING, AND TAX.

TELEPHONE YOUR ORDER BY CALLING OUR 24-HOUR ANSWERING
SERVICE AT 501-536-8221.

ENCLOSED IS MY CHECK OR MONEY ORDER FOR $_____.
(FOR MASTER CARD OR VISA CHARGES, SEE PAGE 160.)

NAME _____

STREET _____

CITY _____ STATE _____ ZIP _____

TELEPHONE NUMBER _____

Charge to my: ☐  ☐ VISA

Account Number:

☐☐☐☐☐☐☐☐☐☐☐☐☐☐   ☐☐☐☐

Expiration Date: _____

Customer's Signature: _____

Please watch for other Southern Flavors Publications and Products!!